The Spark of Enterprise

The Spark of Enterprise

A History of Dixie Foundry–
Magic Chef, Inc.

By

JOHN LONGWITH

MAGIC CHEF, INC.

Cleveland, Tennessee

1988

First American Edition

Library of Congress Catalog Number 87–91291
ISBN 0–944897–00–2

DESIGNED BY WILLIAM MCINTOSH AND JON CORNWELL

*Manufactured in the United States of America
by Arcata Graphics, Kingsport, Tennessee*

Contents

Preface

NOT MANY SMALL, family-owned businesses grow into major American corporations. This book is the authorized history of one that did: Dixie Foundry Company, which the world has come to know as Magic Chef, Inc.

The company has always travelled light, making do with a minimum of staff, perquisites, and offices—a practice that undoubtedly explains why the corporate archive contains precious little, at least up to 1948. Because of the scarcity of written records, I have largely relied for my facts on dozens of persons who consented to interviews. I am grateful to those who generously shared with me their recollections: A. D. (Dick) Adair, Jr., H. S. Albritton, Nelle Askins, Clyde L. Beaty, Bill Burch, James A. Burchett, August Burger, Lee Clemmer, Earl F. Colloms, Willard Corbit, David Dethero, Ruth Dethero, Charles Dickas, George Driscoll, Pauline Dunckel, L. A. Evans, J. T. Greene, Dan Hanks, Betty Harvey, A. W. Herndon, Frederick Heselmeyer, Harvey Hill, and Glover Hogg.

Also to: Charlie Huskey, Giles Huskey, Roy Jarrett, Kitty Johnston, Harold Lauderback, Harold Logan, Robert J. Long, Jr., Bill McClure, Elizabeth Milne, Harold J. Moss, Mrs. Willis Newman, Woody Oden, Harold Ogle, John A. Olsson, Nick Oriti, Charles Owenby, Frederick Nipper, Walter Robinson, Bill Roe, J. Hoyle Rymer, LeRoy Rymer, Jr., Robert

Rymer, Mrs. S. B. Rymer, Sr., S. B. Rymer, Jr., Nelle Sample, Dick Snyder, Roy Steeley, Ron Swanson, Elise Turner, and Anna Ruth Ward.

Others deserve special mention. In Chicago, the staff of the Association of Home Appliance Manufacturers (AHAM) allowed me access to their collection of historical material on the appliance industry. The appliance business is probably the least-chronicled of America's principal industries, but AHAM has gathered the fragmentary accounts into a storehouse of hard-to-find information. Without it, I could not have placed Dixie's development in the context of events taking place in the appliance industry. Many thanks to AHAM's Joyce Viso, Robert Holding, Dorie Nelson, and Mary Johnson.

My greatest debt is to Skeet Rymer, who is the company's institutional memory. All together, I talked with Rymer for more than fifty hours, during which time he often spoke with a frankness that made my task easier than it might otherwise have been. He has done his dead level best to keep me from embarrassing myself.

August 1987   J. L.

PRESS ON

Nothing in the World can take
The place of persistence.

Talent will not;
Nothing is more common than
Unsuccessful men with talent.

Genius will not;
Unrewarded genius is almost
A Proverb.

Education will not;
The world is full of educated
Derelicts.

Persistence and determination
Alone are omnipotent.

—sign in Skeet Rymer's office

The Spark of Enterprise

1.

First Heat

INSIDE THE DARK and airless building on the south side of Cleveland, Tennessee, the cupola furnace squatted heavily over a hole in the earth, its pot belly churning with fire and iron. From the charging platform above, a barechested workman crunched his shovel into a mound of coking coal and, pivoting smoothly, sent the coke clattering down the cupola's shaft.

He had been shoveling since daylight, building a layer-cake of combustibles: coke, pig iron and crushed limestone, more coke, and so on, layer upon layer. The blazing pyre rose up the shaft almost to his feet.

Extending twenty paces out from the cupola was a dirt floor, flat except for the parallel rows of loamy sand running its length. The sand came up to mid-calf on the men who were working in it like farmers in a plowed field. They sifted the sand in sieves and packed it inside two-piece, wooden boxes that opened and closed on hinges. Working the boxes like presses, they shut them on oddly shaped pieces of aluminum that, when removed, left hollow cavities inside the sand-filled boxes.

The men were molders, planters of cast iron. They practiced a craft that the ancient Greeks had venerated in Hephaestus, the lame god of fire and furnace, who was said to have raised the palaces on Olympus and forged the armor of Achilles.

1

But more down-to-earth designs occupied these molders on this morning of July 16, 1917. When they poured iron into their wooden boxes, it would harden into ordinary necessities—the sort of implements a person usually considered beneath notice unless that person happened to be without them: skillets, frying pans, and ham boilers weighing upward of twenty-eight pounds; fireplace grates, andirons—still known as *dog irons*, though canine figures seldom adorned them any longer; boiling pots the size of cauldrons; and flatirons, often called *sad irons*—sad in the antique sense of heavy, though laundresses swore the name perfectly described the experience of using these ten-pound wrinkle smoothers.

As the ironware took shape, so would a business. For ten months it had been a corporate shell, as empty as the cavities inside the wooden boxes. Since its incorporation on August 28, 1916, the Dixie Foundry Company had remained no more than an idea fixed in the head of a Cleveland merchant named Bradford Rymer.

Rymer was on hand for this event. Occasionally he eyed the pressure gauge on the cupola and took a dip of Bruton's snuff. When the molders made indelicate references to one another's manhood or ancestry—not always in anger but more often out of a rough comradeship—Rymer seemed not to hear. Rarely would anybody hear him utter an expletive stronger than "Shucks!" A compact figure just under medium height, Rymer joshed the men in his folksy, slightly bashful manner, and they grinned back appreciatively. Although only thirty-seven, he would soon be known around the foundry as Uncle Brad.

Rymer was present mainly as an observer. The role of iron-master belonged to a burly, mustachioed man from Rome, Georgia—Jefferson Davis Hanks. Rymer called him Dave, and in talking of this occasion the two used a phrase with roots buried deep in a lost Germanic language. They spoke of "drawing the first heat."

Most commercial enterprises are said to "go into business" or to "set up shop." Not so a foundry. Here, the moment of inception is precisely defined. A foundry dates its existence from the drawing of its first heat, an event as rich in symbolism as a farm's first harvest or a ship's maiden voyage. In colonial America, it was customary for a foundryman's wife to light the furnace and, as the flames leaped up, for a bystander to snatch one of her shoes, which he returned only after she had treated all hands to a sumptuous feast.

No such festivity marked the birth of Dixie Foundry. Nobody brought a camera to record the event or a speech to celebrate it. If anybody sensed history in the making, he never said so publicly, not even decades later when hindsight could have conjured up a day of destiny. For his own part, Rymer thought only of keeping the foundry running from one day to the next, and of that he had little assurance. The technical know-how, the patterns for ironware, the day's production— all these belonged to Dave Hanks, who had leased the idle Dixie Foundry from Rymer because striking molders had shut down his own foundry in Georgia, the Hanks Stove & Range Company. It was a makeshift arrangement, but where Rymer came from the choices had usually boiled down to that: either make do or do without.

On the molding room floor, the rows of sand were slowly vanishing, replaced by rows of finished boxes.

Less than twenty-five miles separated Dixie Foundry from Greasey Creek, a speck on the map where the southeastern corner of Tennessee butts together with Georgia and North Carolina in the foothills of the Great Smoky Mountains. It was a land of fatback and molasses, of homespun clothes and homebrewed busthead, of hospitality and homicidal feuds, a land of isolation that some regarded as less than splendid. Born there in 1879, Brad Rymer had spent the better part of his youth looking for a way out of the solitude.

The itch for new places ran in the family. Beginning in the early eighteenth century, successive generations of Rymers had migrated ever westward, impelled by promises of free land as much as by the lack of immediate prospects. They came up from the Rhineland to London and stayed there long enough to book passage to the colony of North Carolina. In 1800, one David Rymer settled on a hundred acres in the Blue Ridge mountains outside Asheville. Over the next thirty years he built up a homestead, which his descendants sold off piece by piece. A 125-acre parcel went to George Washington Vanderbilt, who was amassing 120,000 acres on which to erect a 250-room French Renaissance castle, Biltmore House. By then, however, one branch of the family had already moved deeper into the wilderness, arriving at Greasey Creek, Tennessee, about 1840. It was there that Eli Rymer and Malinda Eveline Mitchell married and set up housekeeping in 1868.

Of the six children born to Eli and Malinda, only Brad and his elder brother Boyd survived past age eight. The family was small compared to most neighboring ones, and the two brothers drew all the closer for that. In a photograph of 1893, Brad and Boyd stand shoulder to shoulder on the plank porch outside their cabin door, facing the camera in identical stances: arms tensed at their sides, hands half balled into fists, grimly looking down as if prepared to meet an approaching war party.

Ambition sealed their bond of kinship. It showed in the little businesses they worked up and managed to run without letting fraternal differences stand in the way of profits. In 1892, when Boyd was nineteen and Brad thirteen, they built a trading post of riven clapboards across from the family cabin. With fifty dollars borrowed from his mother, Boyd stocked its shelves with the essentials of mountain commerce: overalls, hats, shoes, flour, salt, sugar, Brown Mule plug tobacco, and Duke's smoking tobacco. These they swapped for mountain currency—chickens, eggs, game, grain, honey, the odd Mason jar of corn liquor—which they would haul over wagon trails on three-day trips to market in Cleveland, sleeping nights in livery stables or underneath the wagon, and returning with cash and new stock. After six years, the fifty-dollar investment had multiplied into one thousand dollars.

In 1899 Brad and Boyd closed down the trading post and took to the logging business. The quickening pace of industrialization had created a lucrative market in timber, and the forests around Greasey Creek were a storehouse of virgin wood for lumber, fuel, mining props, and railroad ties. Buying timber on the stump, the Rymer brothers had it felled, sawed into boards at mills assembled on the site, and carted to the railroad spur in nearby Reliance, where it brought eight dollars a thousand board feet. But the timber market proved short-lived, at least for small businessmen. As railroads snaked deeper into the mountains, giant lumber companies followed, establishing sawmills and camps close to the source of timber. Around 1900, a Cincinnati-based corporation, the Conasauga Lumber Company, set up operations on more than 65,000 acres of white pine and poplar forests in and around Greasey Creek. Lumber barons now commanded the field.

Trading on their knowledge of the area's timberlands, the

Rymers might have hired on as agents of Conasauga Lumber. Or, like hundreds of other locals, they might have found steady wages in neighboring Copperhill, where the Tennessee Copper Company was about to begin mining and smelting on an unprecedented scale. But Brad and Boyd had not scratched out profits for nine years with the idea of accepting wages at the first opportunity.

They had spent those nine years saving for the day when they could turn their backs on Greasey Creek. Filial devotion had kept them from leaving earlier. But they had put aside capital, and when Eli Rymer died in May of 1901, patriarchal authority passed to the brothers. They were free to set the family's course. They chose a westward route leading to the Oklahoma Territory.

The brothers were drawn there by the same lure that had sent twenty thousand ragtag settlers racing by wagon and buggy or on horseback across the border from Kansas at high noon on April 22, 1889. Homestead 160 acres for five years, and the land was theirs.

On July 22, 1902, three weeks before the family set out for the Oklahoma Territory, Brad Rymer took a bride. Her name was Clara LaDosky Gee, and she was to be Brad's unwavering supporter through thick and thin. The youngest of eight children, Clara Gee grew up in a cabin not far from where the Rymers lived. Her father, a physician trained in Athens and Chattanooga, Tennessee, had brought the family into the mountains in order to minister to the scattered bands of Cherokees who had escaped forcible removal to the Oklahoma Territory. In payment for his services, Dr. Gee received corn meal, syrup, grain, a pig, or nothing at all. He made ends meet by operating a gristmill, but even with that the Gees lived from hand to mouth. For the child Clara, playing dress up meant fashioning hats and frocks out of big cucumber leaves and wild flowers.

Up to age seven she was, by her own description, a "happy child." Then her father died in a storm, crushed beneath a huge oak limb, and with him died the child in Clara. She shouldered the burdens of an adult, working in the fields alongside her brother Henry after the other children had married and moved away. She took over the housework when her mother's health deteriorated. Worse than the grinding labor, though, was the stigma that seemed to go with it. "You'll have to be careful what you do," her mother repeatedly warned Clara and Henry. "You're poor children, and when a poor child gets a stain on his character, it's hard to get clean again."

Clara choked on the idea that she bore some incipient mark of Cain. She "got to hating" her home and "wishing desperately to leave." If Henry teased her about the attentions that one local swain or another paid her, she would snap: "I won't marry any boy who won't take me a thousand miles out of these mountains!"

When at seventeen she left as Brad Rymer's wife, Clara brought to their marriage a burning determination to succeed. Eight years of dogged work had done nothing to dim her spirit. It would help see them through the rough times ahead.

The couple, together with Boyd and mother Malinda, settled on 160 acres of farmland in the Oklahoma Panhandle, near the town of Thomas. From the first, they began to sense that they had made a mistake in coming to the raw prairielands. Coronado, the Spanish explorer who traveled through the Panhandle in 1541, registered something of the amazement that the Rymers must have felt upon first seeing the featureless terrain devoid of perspective. Wrote Coronado: "One can see the sky between the legs of a buffalo, and if a man lay on his back, he lost sight of the ground." The Rymers, accustomed to mountains, were put off by a terrain so flat that it created mirages on the wavering horizon.

The wind unnerved them most of all. It kicked up sand devils and blew tumbledweeds to and fro. On gusty days, sand swirled over their fields, burying seedlings and young plants—a freak of climate that later caused the Panhandle to be tagged the Dust Bowl.

After two months, the family decided to call it quits. Returning to Greasey Creek was more than they could bear, so they made plans to relocate in Cleveland, Tennessee, though no definite prospect awaited them there. Boyd and Malinda, both ill, departed at once, leaving Brad and Clara behind. The couple worked for more than a year, salvaging what they could from the homestead. That turned out to be less than a penny on the dollar. Of the $1,200 Brad had made in the mountains and taken to Oklahoma, exactly ten dollars and change remained when in April of 1904 he stepped off the train in Cleveland.

He found work there as a sixty-cent-a-day factory hand at the Milne Chair Company, and the family—which included Boyd, Malinda, and new-born Zola Marine—crowded into rented quarters. Clara took in piecework from the Hardwick Woolen Mill, sewing pants of an evening. When court was in session, she converted more of her spare time into money by catering meals for the jurors. On Sunday afternoons she and Brad entertained themselves by strolling up and down the rows of stately houses on North Ocoee Street, imagining the house they would build once they had saved ten thousand dollars.

Sometimes reality administered cruel shocks, reminding

them how fragile were their dreams. One morning Clara asked her husband to buy a box of salt on his way home from the chair factory. That evening he stopped off at a corner grocery and asked for the salt on credit. But the clerk insisted on cash.

It was about this time that Brad affixed an *S* before his name, becoming S. Bradford Rymer. The *S* stood for nothing but *S*. It was purely ornamental, like a curlicue added to a signature. But Rymer undoubtedly felt the need to dress up a name that could not command a box of salt. He retained the letter all his life and passed it on to a son.

Another affront to dignity came about 1906 when he went to a Cleveland bank and with hat in hand applied for a loan. With the proceeds, he and his brother Boyd meant to open a grocery, Rymer explained to the banker seated across the desk. After hearing him out, the banker asked, "What collateral do you have?"

"I have got my good name," Rymer replied, assuming that his word was his bond.

"I'm sorry," the banker said, with no trace of sorrow in his voice, "but that won't be good enough."

Swallowing his pride, Rymer found an uncle in Greasey Creek upon whose endorsement the banker agreed to lend the money. The result, Rymer's Grocery, was the first in a series of businesses, each a little larger than the last, which enabled Brad and Boyd to build capital and in 1908 to organize the Cleveland Coal & Feed Company. The company thrived, primarily because of the brothers' foresight in locating it close to a railroad trestle—a placement that allowed them to offload coal with economical speed and thus underprice less favorably situated competitors.

Although Cleveland Coal & Feed was the leading vendor

of coal in Cleveland by 1916, this distinction came too late for Boyd, who had died two years earlier at age forty-one, crippled by arthritis. Together the brothers had created their first solid commercial success in twenty-two years as business partners. Brad would always say, "Boyd could make more money sitting on a stool with his ledgers than I could working." But others remembered Boyd as the more conservative of the two.

There was, in any case, a shade more boldness than caution in the business proposition that Rymer accepted in the early summer of 1916. He agreed to put up $5,000 to start a foundry in partnership with a seasoned but out-of-work ironmaster, J. C. McKenzie, recently let go by Cleveland's Hardwick Stove Company. In theory, Rymer stood to profit more by manufacturing goods than by retailing them through Cleveland Coal & Feed. And the outbreak of war in Europe increased the odds in favor of success. America's iron and steel industry was running at ninety percent of capacity and still falling behind on orders from the war front for barbed wire, shell steel and shrapnel; a new foundry would be entering a seller's market glutted with business.

On the other hand, Rymer lacked the technical skills needed to operate a foundry. This drawback became a considerable liability when J. C. McKenzie died suddenly in November of 1916. Rymer himself could not hope to acquire the vital knowledge that had died with McKenzie. Iron molding was a craft accessible only to those who had been born or apprenticed to it. Ironmasters, observed one authority, "carefully guarded their secrets, which were their most valuable possessions. Ways of making good castings and tricks of furnace management were passed down from father to son, and what technology existed was in the brains of those who excelled, not in any printed form."

Three months passed during which Rymer searched for an ironmaster willing to take McKenzie's place. No likely candidates emerged. At this point Rymer could have backed off with minimal losses, since his expenses thus far had amounted to only a fraction of the $5,000 originally pledged. Instead, he poured money into the foundry. He bought a two-acre site on what had once been the palatial estate of Captain Julius E. Raht—coppermining magnate, banker, and in the 1880s reputedly "the richest man in Tennessee." Since Raht's death, the estate had been sold and subdivided into a patchwork of fields dotted here and there with small houses and factories. At the angle formed by King Edward Avenue and a Southern Railway spur, Rymer erected a tin-roofed building sixty feet long by sixty feet wide.

In the spring of 1917 Rymer organized a board of directors. He also bought a second-hand cupola furnace, though there still was no one to operate it. But by then Rymer was building on faith.

While the molders were completing the last of their wooden boxes, Dave Hanks tripped a switch behind the cupola. With a roar that reverberated like thunder off the corrugated tin roof, a blower cut on, forcing air into the cupola. Waves of shimmering heat rolled off its boilerplate sides as temperatures inside rose to the melting point of iron.

Thirty minutes later, on this July afternoon, Hanks rang an iron bell. In response, the molders lined up before the cupola, sweat streaming off them, hand-rolled cigarettes dangling from the lips of some, long-handled ladles at the ready. One after another, each man held his ladle beneath the rill of molten iron flowing from the cupola. Catching a ladleful, each man carried it with a rhythmic gait onto the molding room floor and poured it into one of his wooden boxes.

For more than an hour the molders shuttled between cupola and boxes, drawing the first heat of Dixie Foundry. Never had Brad Rymer—or anyone else in Cleveland, for that matter—started a business that would go anywhere near so far as the one he now watched take shape.

2.

Plain Grit

A S BRAD AND CLARA RYMER'S seven children were
growing up, they sometimes went days without seeing
their father. Except on Sundays, he usually left home before
Clara roused the children at six in the morning, and he was
often still gone when she put them to bed at eight in the
evening. It was not wide-ranging interests that drew Rymer
away; he belonged to no civic or fraternal organizations other
than the Masons, and the society he liked best was that of
his own family. During those long absences Rymer devoted
himself exclusively to Dixie Foundry. He worked early and
late and, for the first years, all but alone.

There were, in fact, more corporate offices than officers
to fill them. So Rymer simultaneously held down the posts
of president, general manager, and treasurer. He did manage
to recruit as vice-president a person whose skills the company
needed badly. A month after the first heat, Jefferson Davis
Hanks agreed to become an owner of Dixie Foundry rather
than merely rent its plant. With the addition of Hanks, Dixie
gained the technical resources with which to produce its own
line of ironware. Rounding out the short list of stockholders
were Oscar P. Brown, a bookkeeper at Peoples Bank; James
S. O'Neal, corporate secretary; and O'Neal's brother John.
The O'Neals, like Rymer, had come from Greasey Creek
and set up as merchants in Cleveland.

In the beginning Dixie operated as a job shop, going into production one week and out the next, depending on the ebb and flow of orders. As a producer of small batches at irregular intervals, the company was but once removed from a cottage industry. It was a roughhewn business where distinctions between labor and management were not always apparent. President Rymer could often be found alongside the laborers shoveling coke or loading trucks with merchandise. In fact, there were few if any details that Rymer considered beneath him. He ran a bank out of his back pocket; to tide workers over until payday, he lent them small sums—a practice known as "doughballing." Waste was a cardinal sin that Rymer rooted out with a crusader's zeal. A leaky faucet was sure to engage his immediate attention, and he regularly combed the foundry for stray scraps of material that could be re-used. To Rymer, thriftiness was next to godliness, but, then, as one of his children would say, "there wasn't much to waste back then."

At the end of 1918, after its first full year of business, Dixie Foundry netted $5,547.24 for its five stockholders. They decided to plow those profits back into operations, noting in their minutebook that "it was not thought advisable to pay a dividend, as the money would be needed in increasing the capacity of the plant." The booming economy dictated expansion—as much of it as the stockholders could afford. War in Europe had kept the nation's iron and steel industry roaring for three straight years, and even though the guns had fallen silent, the demand for all categories of ferrous goods continued to outstrip the supply. American enamelware exports, having amounted to only $421,000 in 1913, had climbed steadily in volume and value and were now approaching four million dollars.

Under the circumstances, it was a good bet that every dollar spent on increasing Dixie's output would soon reappear with interest on the company's bottom line. All the same, Rymer took a considerable personal risk when, toward the end of 1918, he sold his Cleveland Coal & Feed Company—the one proven success of his business life—and invested the proceeds in Dixie Foundry. He was exchanging the security of an established business for the danger—and possible rewards—of a speculative venture. Not since leaving for the Oklahoma Territory had he played for such high stakes as he would now.

The infusion of capital boosted Dixie's output of what were among the minimal necessities of domestic comfort in 1919. There were Dixie No. 3 dog irons, weighing twenty-four pounds and selling for fifty-four cents a pair. There were skillets, the largest of which—a No. 9—contained five pounds of cast iron and sold for fifty cents. Dixie's English pots, cauldron-shaped vessels balanced on stubby legs, ranged in capacity from eight to twenty gallons and were equally handy for cooking stews, boiling clothes, or making lye soap. The company's line of sugar kettles, which ended with an eighty-pounder of thirty-gallon capacity, sold briskly in Louisiana and Cuba, where they were used to evaporate sugarcane. And there were Dixie muffin pans, hollow ware, sad irons, grates fancy and plain, tea kettles, griddles, and corn stick pans as well.

Rymer also used the fresh capital to finance production of Dixie's first appliance—a wood-burning heater. It represented a logical advance in Dixie's product line. As pieces of engineering, pots and grates were relatively simple to fabricate, since they were of one-piece construction and had no moving parts. In their manufacture, the company had shown basic competence in casting ironware. The heater, with its dampers and doors and other moving parts, presented the next level of engineering difficulty. That mastered, the company would go on to produce, in 1924, a cannon heater, so called because its tall, rounded shape reminded some people of a cannon stood on its breech. To others, its bulging midsection suggested the name by which it is best known: the potbellied stove. Originally mass produced in the early nineteenth century, it had usurped the fireplace as provider of warmth in railroad stations, school houses, general stores, and other public buildings.

J. D. Hanks supplied the prototype, thus removing the hurdle of designing a heater from scratch. It was a model that the Hanks Stove & Range Company sold as the "Jumbo"—an apt name considering that it accepted chunks of stove wood up to three feet in length. With slight modifications in design, Hanks's Jumbo became Dixie's Bigwood Box Heater.

Hanks had long since reopened his own foundry in Rome, Georgia, the strike there having ended. This placed him and Rymer in a somewhat awkward situation: each was selling many of the same goods in much the same territory as the other. Granted, so long as Hanks Stove & Range dwarfed Dixie Foundry, the latter's gain would not necessarily be the former's loss. But as Dixie grew, speeded along by Vice-president Hanks, the potential for intra-company clashes grew as well. Rymer, however, was careful not to become over dependent on the cooperation of a competitor, albeit one who was also a business associate.

As a first step toward making Dixie self-sufficient, Rymer hired a seasoned ironmaster named William Rohlman. A powerfully built man who barked orders in a voice thick with the gutteral consonants of his German homeland, Rohlman took charge of the molding room where he exerted all the authority of a medieval guildmaster. He needed all the authority he could muster, for molders wore the collar of industrial discipline with poor grace, as any number of unvarnished accounts attest. Colonel William Byrd, after visiting a foundry in Virginia, wrote that the molders "find it very hot work to tend the furnace, especially in summer, and are obliged to spend no small part of their earnings in strong drink to recruit their spirits." And an entry in the log of one nineteenth-century foundry read: "Blew the furnace at 8 o'clock P.M. All hands drunk."

An ironmaster who could keep a crew of molders in the traces was worth his weight in gold. To this task Rohlman brought the sort of knowledge likely to earn him the men's respect: tricks of cupola tending, of sand mixing, of casting. And if knowledge alone failed to back up his authority, he never hesitated to trade profanities with the molders, and he was equally ready to joke or to fight with them. One measure of Rohlman's value to Dixie was evident in 1920 when Rymer named him a director.

A prosperous economy had given Rymer the opening to expand Dixie, but that opening began to close like a noose in the spring of 1919. Prices suddenly skyrocketed, pushing the cost of living up 105 percent above the pre-war level. Milk, which had sold for nine cents a quart in 1914, cost fifteen cents. The same pound of butter that had once cost thirty-two cents went for sixty-one cents. To make matters worse, wages lagged behind prices. Watching their money lose value, people ruefully remarked that even the man without a dollar to his name was fifty cents better off than he once was. Because installment lending had not yet become a popular means of disguising inflation's damage to purchasing power, most people were left with no alternative but to curb their spending. The result was what economists termed the "buyers' strike" of 1919.

The buyers' strike caught Dixie on the wrong foot, expanding in a contracting economy. Orders began to fall off, and by early summer the company's increased capacity lay idle. To make matters worse, Rymer was stuck with dead inventory, particularly sugar kettles, which had to be sold at a loss. More and more often, Bill Rohlman greeted arriving molders with the announcement: "No work today, boys. Come back tomorrow." In July, one of Dixie's bank accounts registered a negative balance of $10.17.

Winter, the one season when a stove maker such as Dixie could count on moving merchandise, brought little relief. Ordinarily, the demand for stoves rose as the mercury fell, but during the winter of 1919–1920 a worsening economy flattened sales of the company's Bigwood Box Heater. That winter many people dropped the term buyers' strike and adopted another one—depression. Although mild in comparison to the financial panics of 1873 and 1893, the depression of 1920 lingered on into 1921.

The hard times tested Rymer's commitment to Dixie Foundry. Two of his directors, the O'Neal brothers, resigned from the company, and he found it impossible to replace them with anyone willing to buy a block of shares even at bargain prices. J. B. Brown, brother of Oscar Brown, joined the board but put up only a token investment; Clara Rymer was pressed into service to fill the other vacancy on the board.

Unofficially, Dixie was bankrupt early in 1920, when Rymer placed a late night telephone call to W. H. Albritton, the new owner of Cleveland Coal & Feed as well as a boyhood friend from Greasey Creek. He would lose the foundry, Rymer told Albritton, unless he raised money immediately. Rymer mentioned his most valuable remaining asset, the main building of Cleveland Coal & Feed. He offered to sell it at a good price to Albritton and his partner, John L. Jones. After further talk the next day, Rymer sold the building to the two businessmen. With the proceeds, he replenished Dixie's bank account, retrieving the company from ruin. But it was a close call—a fact that Rymer acknowledged decades later when he allowed that he "nearly went broke" before the worst was over.

3.

Peaks and Valleys

FOR A MAN who watched his pennies as if they were dollars, a man who could not long abide the sight of a leaky faucet, Brad Rymer was anything but tightfisted with risk capital. His borrowings to keep Dixie afloat through the recession of 1920 had been sizable. But even before he had got out from under those debts he began piling up new ones. This time, he needed the money to build a new product—cooking ranges.

Producing ranges was a natural, if financially burdensome, move for Rymer. Many of Dixie's products had aged noticeably since 1917. And now, early in 1921, the aging process had accelerated as a new generation of appliances entered the nation's homes, forever changing American housework.

Electric irons were replacing sad irons, which, to the regret of few users, were relegated to duty as doorstops or fireplace ornaments. Rust-free cooking utensils of aluminum, enameled cast iron, and pyrex were crowding hollow ware out of kitchen cabinets. Vacuum cleaners, which virtually eliminated the arduous chore of moving rugs outside and beating them clean, exerted more sales appeal than did the humble box heater.

The basic technology needed to build these goods had been around a while. Irons were electrified in 1903, enameled cookware was sold as early as 1874, and the vacuum cleaner was first patented in 1901. What had been missing, though, were

20

techniques of mass production and mass distribution that could deliver these goods by the trainloads at affordable prices. The breakthrough in production had come in 1914, when Henry Ford installed the first moving assembly line with an endless-chain conveyer. It cut the assembly time of a Model T from 14 hours to 93 minutes, and the price from $950 to $360.

Emulating Ford, appliance makers began producing a flood of housewares after World War I. Leading the list were electric irons and vacuum cleaners, followed by toasters, oil furnaces, mixers (called "electric egg beaters"), ranges, coffee percolators, "frigidaires," and washing machines. These enjoyed prominent display in the store windows and catalogs of a rapidly expanding network of retailers—notably chain stores—which grew in number from 29,000 in 1918 to 160,000 in 1929. Public utilities were growing too, extending the powerlines and pipelines that supplied energy to millions of new appliance owners.

The revolution in production and consumption would make antiques of many familiar household goods. Obsolescence clearly awaited such products as Dixie's sad irons and hollow ware, and it was to compensate for their eventual loss that Rymer planned to develop a line of coal and wood-burning ranges.

His decision came at a time when several large appliance makers were already shifting their production from coal-and-wood burners to the more popular gas range. But Dixie, possessing little capital and less engineering knowledge, was in no position to undertake the manufacture of gas ranges. Coal-and-wood ranges, on the other hand, offered a natural step up the product ladder, since they represented a level of engineering difficulty between box heaters and gas ranges.

Still, Dixie's resources allowed no margin for serious mistakes or for much research and development. Ranges would have to pay their way by the time that the loans covering start-up costs fell due. Every bit of cash flow mattered dearly, and in 1921, when work began on the line, Rymer slashed his salary to $2,488 for the year. The situation was more precarious than two directors could accept. At the board meeting of June 28, the brothers Oscar and J. B. Brown took leave of Dixie. Rymer bought their stock, replacing them on the board with A. H. Rogers, superintendant of Hanks Stove & Range, and William Rohlman, Dixie's own crusty overlord of molding. Later, in a conversation with Rymer's wife Clara, Oscar Brown made a Delphic prophesy: "Brad's either going to be a rich man or a poor man one day."

Dixie's cooking range started out as a freehand drawing. Because blueprints were unknown at the company, the drawing alone served as a rough guide for constructing a lead prototype. The prototype was delivered to the model shop where it was converted into wood master patterns by a quiet, gentlemanly man by the name of General White. People who remember White insist that he was more than an ace whittler: "General was a genius with wood," said one.

The test of White's skill came once the prototype had passed inspection, which simply meant, according to one observer, that everybody agreed it "looked right." At this point, White painstakingly carved slabs of oak into master patterns for each of the range's several dozen parts. From these handmade patterns, workers would construct aluminum replicas known as matchplates. What dies are to metal stamping, matchplates were to iron casting. Molders would place a matchplate between two layers of tightly packed sand held in a special hinged box called a flask, which worked something like a waffle iron. By closing the flask then opening it and removing the matchplate, a molder formed inside the flask an impression in sand. Snap the flask shut, pour in molten gray iron, and the result was a perfectly shaped part—provided that, among other things, General White's master patterns were true. And it was only after assembling the finished parts that White and Rymer could know whether the design that looked right actually was right.

The engineering depended largely on craftsmanship rather than on applied science; people worked with their hands and sharp tools rather than with sliderules and blueprints. Production demanded an even greater expenditure of labor, since over 300 pounds of cast iron and steel went into every stove. Setting to work before daylight, men pitched pig iron and shoveled coking coal into the cupola furnace—itself a giant stove. While the mixture melted, molders were busy putting together the sand-filled flasks into which iron would be poured.

By one o'clock, all was in readiness for what was called the "tapping out." Rows of assembled flasks stretched up and down the molding room floor. Inside the cupola, the temperature hovered at 2700 degrees Fahrenheit, heating the room to 100 degrees or better even in the dead of winter. Using a long steel pole, a man worked loose the clay plug in the cupola's wall where a waist-high sluiceway branched off. Out rushed a stream of liquid iron, incandescent orange and hypnotic to watch. Lined up where the sluiceway ended in a spout, the molders, many of them stripped to the waist, caught the fiery liquid in long-handled ladles and carried those 60-pound loads to their flasks. If so much as a few drops spilled out along the way, a shower of burning sparks erupted, pinwheeling in all directions.

The smell of burning sulphur hung in the air. Smoke rose from the cooling molds, inside which expanding gases sometimes exploded with the pop and crack of muffled gunfire. In full swing, the molding room resembled an industrial Inferno, peopled with half-naked men, their bodies glistening with sweat and their faces lit up in the flickering orange glow of molten iron.

Later in the day, when the iron had hardened inside the flasks, the "shake out" crew went to work. They moved down the rows of flasks, stooping over like cotton pickers, and freed the range parts from their sand cocoons. In addition to a strong back, the shake-out man needed a pair of quick and sure hands, for the parts were not only heavy—some weighed upwards of 60 pounds—but they were also jagged in places and still hot enough to cause nasty burns.

Ground smooth of burrs, the parts were ready for assembly. This was done by "floor mounters," working at low benches equipped with turntables. They put together a stove the hard way—from the ground up, as if building a house. "If a man assembled ten stoves in a ten-hour day, he had done something," recalled one veteran of the mounting department. The company's first motorized assembly line was still many years in the future.

After final assembly, the ranges were inspected, painted, and crated. Crating, like assembly itself, started from the ground and worked up. A wooden crate bottom was maneuvered underneath the range, vertical sections were nailed into place, and a top was added to complete the structure.

The finished range, unveiled in 1921, was as rugged as the work that had gone into it. Weighing 350 pounds or more, depending on the model, it stood ponderously on iron legs, had six cooking holes and a backpanel topped with warming closets. To use this beast, a cook needed a few things besides culinary skills and a full larder. She needed brute strength to tote in loads of stovewood or coal and to haul out buckets of cinders and ash. She needed the skills of a woodsman to kindle fires, particularly if the wood was wet or the house drafty. She also had to exercise vigilance over the fire, to keep it from flickering out, and once it caught she had to stay clear of the range's outer surfaces as they heated up—a precaution impressed on cooks who were so careless as to lay bare hands on blistering hot door handles or sidepanels.

Properly charged and tended, the range would operate for about four hours before the fire required rekindling. Rymer christened it the Larine, a partial anagram he made from the name of his first child, daughter Zola Marine.

To the untrained eye, the Larine and ranges of similar make may have looked like artifacts as old as flintlock rifles and spinning looms. But, in fact, they were of much more recent vintage. Not until 1846 did the term *cooking range* enter the language, and it was only in 1851, during the presidency of Millard Fillmore, that the first iron kitchen range was put into service at the White House. Before then, presidents and commoners alike ate meals cooked in open fireplaces. As a cooking device, the fireplace left much to be desired. Besides sending most of its heat up the chimney—and sparks into the room—the fireplace did not allow cooks to bake, broil, and simmer several dishes at once. Hence, meals from the fireplace were usually crude affairs, consisting of one dish cooked in one pot.

Early efforts to improve on this sometimes ended badly. The Frenchman Marie-Antoine Carême, considered by many to be the greatest chef of all time, died at the relatively early age of 49, possibly having succumbed to noxious vapors from the primitive coal oven that he had rigged up. Indeed, one eulogy to Carême said that he had been "burned out by the flame of his genius and the fumes of his ovens."

The cast-iron range, first advertised in 1741 as an "iron fireplace," offered thermal efficiency, safety, and cooking possibilities far beyond anything obtainable from even the best fireplace. But it was not until after the Civil War that cooking ranges began to appear in sufficient numbers to influence American cooking.

Although designed more for durability than for elegance or ease of operation, the Dixie Larine did offer housekeepers some fairly new conveniences. Its enameled finish was an advance over bare cast iron, which rusted without liberal applications of stove polish and elbow grease. A thermometer mounted in the oven door took some of the guesswork out of baking, and an optional water reservoir supplied what was still a scarce commodity in many households: hot water.

Most attractive of all, however, was the fact that the Larine was a good buy in its class and in its price range. A top-of-the-line model could be had for about $40, and there were basic models for under $25—prices usually within the means of the unskilled laborer or small farmer.

The same principles underlying Dixie's first cooking range were to be applied with regularity in the years ahead. The words "sturdy," "practical," and "value" appeared often in Dixie's advertising. Far less frequently used were such words as "beauty," "smart," and "stylish." Seldom would Dixie be the first company, or even the second or third, to market a new product. But when the company did go to market, it was usually with a product that appealed to the cost-conscious customer who prized function above fashion.

The Larine sold well, so well that in January of 1923 Rymer decided to operate the plant full-time, or, as the minutes noted, "as nearly so as possible." Instead of calling in workers only when there were enough orders to justify running the plant, Dixie would operate six days a week, ten hours a day. It was an eventful change. In scheduling work by the clock, the company advanced out of the pre-industrial stage of development.

But as output increased, so would pressure to obtain a steady flow of orders. If sales fell off sharply and unexpectedly, it would no longer be so easy to shut down before excess inventory reached dangerous levels. Rymer had given thought to developing an effective sales program but had concluded that he was not the man to do it. Horse trader though he was, Rymer was also a homebody who felt most comfortable with his family and with the country folk whom he knew so well. Once, on a train taking him to Dixie's first show at the Chicago Furniture Market, Rymer was sitting alone when some business acquaintances came up and invited him to join them for lunch in the dining car. "No, I brought mine," he replied, displaying the sack lunch that his wife had packed for him.

As Rymer knew, Dixie needed a sales manager other than himself, someone who would relish going back to that dining car and striking deals over lunch. With this in mind, Rymer had brought into the company a new director and stockholder: Grover Cleveland Brown. A native of Boaz, Alabama, Brown had grown up in an area of hard-scrabble farms and pine barrens known as Sand Mountain. As a young man he had come down from the Alabama hill country to attend business school in Nashville, then settled in Cleveland where he moved up through the ranks of the Hardwick Stove Company to become executive assistant to the town's leading industrialist and most influential citizen, Christopher L. Hardwick. In

September 1921, Brown left Hardwick to accept the post of secretary-treasurer at Dixie. Whatever Brown's title might be, it was evident from the start that his influence within the company would be second only to Rymer's. Each man drew the same salary and agreed to equal raises thenceforth. Rymer promised to sell Brown additional stock. And when money was raised to operate the foundry full-time, both men stood good for the loans.

Their business relations inched closer in 1924. At the board meeting of March 25, attended by both men and directors William Rohlman and A. H. Rogers—J. D. Hanks having left the company at the end of 1923—Brown proposed a major reorganization. He moved that Dixie surrender its corporate charter "at the earliest date possible" and do business as a "partnership in the future," a partnership composed of himself and Rymer. Brown's motion, seconded by Rohlman, was passed unanimously. So was another motion to the same effect put forward on April 1st. But no action was taken, not then or during the remainder of 1924.

This curious combination of resolution and inaction, Rymer's children later said, stemmed from a dilemma that Brad Rymer faced. Dixie needed an efficient sales manager and Brown looked like that man, but in return for his contributions Brown insisted on being made a partner—that is, having the same power as Rymer—though his financial stake in the company was far less than Rymer's. This was more than Rymer had intended when he brought Brown into Dixie. But instead of bringing the matter to a head, Rymer temporized, going along with the resolutions to convert to a partnership yet using his majority ownership to block the change.

Dixie remained a corporation through 1925 and 1926, during which years sales grew steadily under Brown's direction.

In 1926, Dixie's sixteen salesmen tallied up sales worth $491,643, and the company showed a year-end profit of $60,062, an increase of some seventeen percent over the previous year.

As sales increased, so did the pressure Brown exerted to convert Dixie to a partnership. Finally Rymer acquiesced. On January 1, 1927, Rymer and Brown began doing business as equals. By the terms of their agreement, dated July 1, 1926, Rymer, together with his wife, owned 78.5 percent of the company and Brown 21.5 percent.

The change had far-reaching implications for Dixie. By converting to a general partnership, Dixie lost its potential to raise capital through stock offerings or to broaden its ownership. More important than that, however, was the fact that Dixie's fate was now tangled up with Brown and Rymer's ability to work in harmony, since each man now had the same say-so in company affairs. If an irreconcilable difference arose, it could no longer be settled by a vote of the stockholders.

Dixie's income and profits held firm through 1927, despite an economic slump at year's end. Then the economy rebounded and took off on a dizzying run. In less than two years' time, the Dow Jones Average would shoot up by 100 percent. Economists predicted that the nation had arrived at a "permanent plateau of prosperity," and the public mood of boundless optimism was reflected in the titles of such popular songs as "We're in the Money," and "It Ain't Gonna Rain No More." When Ford announced the Model A early in 1928, 500,000 people made down payments without having seen the car and without knowing its price. Riding the wave of prosperity, Dixie's sales climbed to $729,892 in 1928, and profits soared to $87,692.

Encouraged by these hefty gains, Rymer and Brown began development of a gas range. It would be Dixie's first modern appliance, designed for the up-to-the-minute kitchen. Natural gas itself had been used as a fuel since before Confucius, by Chinese saltmakers who pipelined gas through bamboo tubes to heat their evaporating pans. But its acceptance in America had been slow. Although gas ranges were available to the public in the 1880s, they were not popular. Compared to coal- or wood-burning stoves, the gas range was cooler to operate and its individually controlled burners allowed a cook to prepare small dishes without firing up an entire stove. Nonetheless, most households continued to cook with coal or wood until the turn of the century.

It was then that the gas utilities entered the picture. Crippled by the nation's wholesale conversion from smoky gasoliers to clean electric lighting, the gas utilities faced extinction unless they found new markets for manufactured gas. They soon began to promote gas as the "fuel of the future" for domestic cooking and heating. With this boost from the utilities, a lucrative market developed in gas ranges and heaters. By 1928, as Dixie prepared to enter that market, gas ranges were beginning to supplant coal burning ranges in urban areas.

Coming off the assembly line in 1929, Dixie's range resembled a lighter, streamlined version of the Larine. But as a piece of engineering, the new range was a good deal more complicated than its predecessor. In place of the firebox, dampers, and cooking holes of the Larine, there were burners that might clog, valves and tubing that might leak or freeze up. To help minimize the manufacturing headaches, Rymer and Brown had imported outside talent in the person of Tom Carlock, a gas range builder who came to Dixie from the Vesta Stove Works, of Chattanooga, Tennessee. Later, Fred Nipper would take charge of the gas range division.

In styling as well as in engineering, Dixie's gas range represented a new level of sophistication for the company. Like the Model T, Dixie's earlier products had been available in any color, so long as it was black. But even Ford had surrendered to the popular demand for color, halting production of the Model T in 1927 and replacing it with the Model A, which could be bought in hues ranging from Dawn Gray to Arabian Sand. One appliance manufacturer went so far as to make vermilion-colored refrigerators, decorated with parrots perched on green branches. Another company, American Stove, based in St. Louis, Missouri, had introduced a line of ranges designed to resemble fine furniture—a line the company called Magic Chef. So stylish was the Magic Chef that, according to the home service director of the Montana-Dakota Utility Company, one housewife in North Dakota, declaring her Magic Chef range "too pretty to use," had placed a lace runner on it and was doing her cooking on a hot plate.

Of the rage for style and fashion, the New York *Times* wrote in 1927: "As our bathrooms are changing in spirit from the old, ultra-chaste whiteness to more gracious and gayer interiors, so our kitchens are adding to their efficiency the charm of color. . . . One reason is that the mistress of the house has much more to do with the kitchen in these servantless days than she had heretofore." Another explanation for the trend held that Prohibition, by taking drinking out of the saloon, had led to the custom of having drinks with friends in the kitchen, where "no self-respecting hostess dared have outdated appliances in the foreground."

Whether the shortage of servants or of saloons was behind it, the demand for color in the kitchen was too strong to be safely ignored. Dixie's catalog of gas ranges featured models enameled in white and in combinations of gray, white, ivory, and green.

The Hardwick Stove Company sat on a rise overlooking Dixie Foundry. Because of this location, workers on Hardwick's first shift were distracted from their jobs on the morning of Thursday, February 6, 1929. "Come look! Our competitor is burning down!" cried one worker. Others rushed to the windows to see flames shooting up from Dixie's plant.

The fire spread rapidly, engulfing all the assembly buildings on the east side of King Edward Avenue. Its cause, some later speculated, was a flame or spark given off during the night by one of the 55-gallon heating drums, known as salamanders, that dotted the plant. The alarm had been sounded shortly after 6 a.m. Four hours later, fire engines were still pouring water on hot embers and smoldering walls. A secretary present that morning remembered that as Rymer watched the blaze he "looked like he wanted to cry." But he put on a brave face, telling the press that the ruined buildings had been "more or less of a temporary nature" and that Dixie would be back in operation within ten days. He also fell to work rebuilding. Before the fire engines left, Dixie's molders and floor mounters were already tearing down cooler parts of the gutted buildings. One molder, Jim Taylor, who would later become superintendent of the plant and head of purchasing, recalled putting in "16 hours a day after the fire cleaning up the coal and wood ranges we could salvage."

At least the foundry, offices, and assembly areas on the

west side of King Edward Avenue had been spared. But even after collecting on its fire insurance policy, Dixie sustained a loss of $44,312—a loss that made itself felt on the bottom line. Operations would have yielded a profit of $99,204 in 1929, except that after subtracting the fire loss, profits fell to $54,891, a 37 percent drop from the previous year.

The fire marked a turn for the worse in Dixie's fortunes. Four trying years would pass before the company once again showed an annual profit of $50,000. Toward the end of 1929, Dixie began to sell great quantities of gas ranges on consignment, meaning that a dealer paid for the ranges only after he sold them. The company, in effect, was becoming a banker to its dealers. At the same time, inventory in the warehouse reached unprecedented levels. The combination of high inventory and consignment sales can be risky in the best of times. It proved downright foolhardy in late 1929, when the nation's economy plunged into the longest and deepest depression in America's history.

4.

A Season of Discontent

AUTHORITIES WOULD later differ on precisely when the turning point came, some dating it as early as the Florida Land Bubble of 1925, and others arguing that not until the Big Bull Market of 1928 did America lock into a collision course with disaster. This much was certain: after 1925 the nation's industrial boom turned into a speculative binge as the conviction spread that everybody ought to be rich.

The bandwagon of prosperity, which had taken America to the highest standard of living any people had ever known, originally rolled off the assembly lines of Detroit and other centers of invention and technology. But then it headed into the fantasyland of margin and leverage.

In 1928 the New York Stock Exchange was outperforming all other parts of the economy. Capital and excess profits were pouring into the stock market, driving stock prices higher and higher while industrial output actually levelled off. U.S. Steel shot up from $160 to $268 a share in three months of frenzied trading. Radio Corporation of America leaped from 85 to 420, even though it had never paid a dividend. But an investor who bought ten shares of RCA early that year, putting up $100 on margin and borrowing the rest from his broker, could have sold the shares at year's end for $4,200.

Such miracles were enough to convince millions of people

that somewhere over what one investment firm called the "ever ascending curve of American prosperity," there awaited an inexhaustible pot of gold. "Nothing," declared a business leader, "can arrest the upward movement."

But what if a sizable number of investors decided to take their profits instead of holding out for more? And what if they all picked the same moment to cash in their chips?

When that happened on Thursday, October 24, 1929, the New York Stock Exchange broke, then rallied briefly before collapsing under an avalanche of sell orders. RCA plummeted to 28, and many other stocks could not be unloaded at any price. The repercussions were immediate and disastrous.

Reacting to the crash, business reined in spending, consumers tightened their belts, banks curbed lending, government put the lid on deficit spending, and in no time at all the economy ground to a halt.

From the top of prosperity in early 1929 to the bottom of depression three years later, production fell to less than it had been in 1913. The number of new automobiles coming out of Detroit decreased by eighty percent; steel plants cut back until they were running at only twelve percent of capacity; the output of pig iron dropped to lows not seen since the Panic of 1893. Investment all but ceased, falling from $16.2 billion to $800 million. The gains of a decade were wiped out.

The only ascending curves were those charting human misery. Unemployment soared from 3.2 percent to 24.9 percent, and six million men tramped the streets looking for work, a soup kitchen or a breadline. Another one million men and boys drifted aimlessly across the countryside, riding the rails and living in hobo jungles. Each day over one thousand families lost their homes in foreclosures.

The desperate times stirred men to desperate actions. Groups of angry farmers arrived at foreclosures and, brandishing pitchforks and hangman's nooses, persuaded sheriffs to call a halt to the proceedings. In May 1930 a thousand New Yorkers standing in a breadline suddenly stormed two bakery trucks that were making deliveries at a nearby hotel. Two years later, when 15,000 unemployed veterans descended on Washington and demanded payment of their World War I bonuses, the U.S. Army drove them away with tanks, tear gas, and fixed bayonets.

Taken altogether, it was the worst crisis since the Civil War.

For Cleveland, Tennessee, as for cities and towns across the nation, the Great Depression was the economic equivalent of war. A quiet town of farms, factories, and churches—nineteen churches for a populace of 9,000—Cleveland suffered hardships generally thought to have passed with the Reconstruction Era. Out of an industrial work force 2,300 strong in 1929, about four out of every five men were jobless in 1932, according to a report of the Reconstruction Finance Corporation. The fortunate among them fell back on the surrounding farmlands, where they eked out a living, though just barely, for drought followed by overproduction had sent crop prices tumbling past even the depressed levels of 1929; wheat from $1.05 to 39 cents a bushel, corn from 81 cents to 33 cents a bushel, cotton from 17 cents to 6 cents a pound.

Two of Cleveland's major employers—the Milne Chair Company and the Cleveland Casket Company—closed down entirely in 1932, reducing the list of principal manufacturers to three textile mills, two stove foundries, and an enameling plant. Among the survivors, Dixie Foundry was entering its fourth straight year of declining profits.

The stock market crash had caught Dixie just when it had built up inventory to nearly three times the level of 1928. Those goods, manufactured in the flush of prosperity, had to be sold in the depth of depression. To move the inventory, Brown and Rymer cut prices, often by half or more; one model of the Larine that had sold for $59 in 1920 was reduced to $27.50. Brown also offered customers and distributors liberal terms in exchange for pushing Dixie's merchandise. As a result, the company, through its distributors, sold large quantities of merchandise on consignment or on credit. That preserved Dixie's volume of sales in 1930, though annual earnings fell from the previous $54,892 to $12,027.

The next year sales sagged, and earnings dipped to a mere $4,653. But more disturbing was the loss from accounts so far in arrears as to be deemed uncollectable: $15,097. That figure amounted to ten percent of the total value of accounts due the company. It was a heavy load of bad debt for a business with such slender margins of profit. Or, to put it another way: assuming that Dixie's return on sales again hit the peak of twelve percent reached in 1928, then in order to recoup a loss of $15,000 it would need to sell an additional $125,000 in merchandise, and $125,000 in merchandise translated into 12,820 Bigwood Box heaters or 4,545 deluxe Larines. What the company needed most, however, was not more business but more profitable business.

It ended up with neither in 1932. Orders dried up, and Rymer and Brown laid off workers until only the most senior and most valued remained. Even then, there was not enough work to go around. Molders, who were paid by the job rather than by the hour, sometimes poured as few as two flasks a day, where before they had done as many as fifty. On the rare days when word spread that Dixie was hiring, hundreds of Cleveland's jobless presented themselves outside Dixie's gate in hopes of being called to work as mounters at wages of ten cents an hour. Most left disappointed. From 1929 to 1932, annual wages paid by the company dropped from $246,000 to $122,000.

When the accounts were balanced at the end of 1932, the result was a loss of $6,230 on sales of $614,509. To make matters worse, the new year started off with a wave of bank failures that brought the nation to its knees. By the end of February, 5,504 banks across the nation had closed indefinitely, their deposits of $3.43 billion beyond the reach of desperate customers. Currency virtually disappeared from circulation in many cities, including Atlanta, Knoxville, and Asheville, where workers found inside their pay envelopes not cash but scrip—hastily printed vouchers resembling currency and supposedly as negotiable. But as quite a few workers discovered, some merchants refused to honor scrip except at a discount on its face value.

In Cleveland, money was so scarce that at least two factories—the Hardwick Woolen Mill and the Bacon Hosiery Mill—issued scrip, or "due bills," in lieu of cash wages. To avoid that at Dixie, Rymer once made a quick trip to the Birmingham Trust Company, returning with a satchel containing the cash to meet a payroll in the nick of time.

In February of 1933, with Dixie running in the red and the economy in shambles, Rymer was on the razor's edge of losing all that he had scraped together during fifty-three years of ceaseless work. By the standards of Cleveland, he was a wealthy man. Apart from Dixie Foundry, he owned farmland and several pieces of real estate, not least of which was the stately house on North Ocoee Street that he and Clara had

dreamed of years before. But he was cash poor. On the twenty-
fourth, he borrowed $535.80 against the cash value of his
life insurance policy.

One morning not long after, he and Clara were sitting
over breakfast, talking of business and family matters out of
earshot of the children, as was their habit. "Mother," he
said, reaching over and laying a hand on her shoulder, "it
looks like my obligations are so heavy that I'm going to have
to sell the home." Dry-eyed and unruffled, Clara replied, "If
you have to sell it, Brad, then sell it."

Another year of losses at Dixie, and the family could start
packing. Under the gun now, Rymer squarely faced a question
at the heart of Dixie's performance. How much bad debt
ought Dixie to swallow in promoting sales? As early as 1930
Brown's effort to revive flagging sales with generous doses of
credit had, in the words of the company's auditors, proved
"less than uniformly successful." Orders taken on consignment
or credit had, increasingly, become dead losses to be written off at the end of the year. From $15,097 in 1931, write-
offs had jumped to $24,110 the next year, or twenty-two per-
cent of all accounts receivable. Measured another way, the
write-offs had equaled four percent of sales in 1932. Considering that Dixie's return on sales generally ran well below
ten percent, losses of such magnitude posed a grave problem.

No mutually agreeable solution suggested itself to the two
partners. Concluding that Dixie was too small for the both
of them, Rymer made Brown a proposition: "You either buy
my interest or sell me yours." Brown chose the latter course,
selling Rymer his minority interest on November 29, 1933.
Less than a month later, on December 15, Rymer re-incorpo-
rated the firm as the Dixie Foundry Company. Thus ended

Rymer's first and last experiment in operating the company as a partnership.

The re-organization marked the beginning of a new management era at Dixie. Henceforth, Rymer would rely exclusively on his own family to fill top positions, with the result that in the years ahead a family gathering could be turned into a directors' meeting at a moment's notice, since Dixie's board and the Rymer family were one and the same.

Already, two sons had joined their father at the company. The elder, LeRoy, had arrived in 1927, after attending Kansas State Agricultural College. A gruff bull of a man who never backed away from a fight, LeRoy was tenaciously loyal to his friends, and as one of them remarked: "if he liked you, there wasn't nothing he wouldn't do for you." He served as a strong right arm to his father, and in 1934 he would be named general manager.

The second son to sign on, Marvin, started out in the crating department in 1929. He possessed an easy charm that his father and elder brother lacked. People who remembered Brad and LeRoy as "hard to get to know" also remembered feeling an immediate rapport with Marvin. Affable and dapper, Marvin quickly demonstrated a flair for salesmanship and, in 1933, took charge of Dixie's sales.

Dixie's prospects brightened toward the end of 1933. In mid-year the economy improved noticeably, owing largely to the bold recovery measures adopted by President Franklin Roosevelt during his first one hundred days in office. As the depression eased, Rymer and his sons pulled Dixie out of its four-year slump. Sales increased to $746,000 and returned a profit of $45,000. And by applying rigorous credit standards, Brad Rymer slashed write-offs and continued to hold them down even during adverse years.

The upward trend gained force in 1934, when for the first time sales topped the $1-million mark, and profits exceeded those of the banner year of 1928. Encouraged by this showing, Rymer borrowed $100,000 with which to expand Dixie's line of gas ranges.

The decision to invest more heavily in gas ranges was a fortunate one for the company. The Coal and Wood Age of the appliance industry was almost over, though some stove foundries would make the fatal mistake of offering only coal and wood burners after most of America's kitchens had long since converted to gas or electric ranges. Any tendency for Dixie to lag far behind the times was, however, counteracted by the method of distribution it had chosen around 1930. Before then, the bulk of orders came from many small dealers. Afterwards, sixty-to-seventy percent of sales were made directly to a few large retailers—Montgomery Ward, Spiegel, Firestone Tire and Rubber—which put their own brand names on Dixie's products. Known in the industry as "private labeling," this arrangement compelled Dixie to tailor its line to fit the national markets of chain stores. As Montgomery Ward and the others bought fewer coal and wood burning ranges and more gas fuelled ones, Dixie began to realign its production accordingly.

In 1935 Rymer introduced the new gas range, which was available with ovens of fourteen inches, sixteen inches, and eighteen inches, came in assorted color combinations of green, ivory, and mother of pearl, and varied in price from $32.32 to $57.36. A sales brochure described one model, the Cherokee, as the answer for "Value-conscious Americans who have grown tired of 'junk-at-depression-prices.'" Concluded the appeal: "Here's the biggest dollar's worth of gas range merchandise on the market. Not the cheapest gas range—but most for the money. QUALITY—the average home can afford."

Sales of the range carried profits upward, to slightly over $100,000 in 1935, then to $112,544 by 1937. That year, however, the momentum abuilding since 1933 slowed when, in quick succession, labor unrest flared and then the economy took a bad spill.

Industrialists in Cleveland, like their counterparts elsewhere, had forcefully and successfully opposed the labor union movement since its rise in the 1880s. When during the 1890s a strike had broken out at Cleveland's Hardwick Stove Company, a youthful C. L. Hardwick had wired his father asking what to do should the company be forced to sue for peace. Back came the reply: "Burn it down and plant it in turnips." To lose a campaign against the unions was to lose all.

But that uncompromising stand had never been put to the test, for the courts had invariably ruled strikes illegal and ordered the arrest of organizers who defied injunctions. When the International Moulders Union (IMU) launched a strong drive at Dixie in the early thirties, a local court had issued a "permanent and perpetual" injunction against the union.

Then, in the summer of 1935, Congress handed labor a powerful new weapon, the Wagner Act, otherwise known as the National Labor Relations Act. It created a National Labor Relations Board empowered not only to prohibit unfair practices by employers who sought to block unionization but also to declare and conduct elections to determine if workers wished to bargain collectively and, if so, to make their decision binding on the employer. Government, long an ally of business in labor disputes, became an active neutral.

The labor movement, its hand strengthened, took to the

offensive. Spearheading it was the Congress of Industrial Organizations (CIO), formed in 1935 by John L. Lewis and other
labor leaders whom the American Federation of Labor (AFL)
had ousted for recruiting mass-production workers instead of
limiting membership to craft workers. Backed by the CIO,
workers at dozens of plants shut down assembly lines and
refused to leave the premises while union officials negotiated
with management; in May 1937 there were 170 sit-down
strikes involving 167,210 workers. These strikes wrung un-
heard-of concessions from some of the nation's industrial giants: General Motors, RCA, Firestone Tire and Rubber, General Electric, and U.S. Steel.

Emboldened by these victories, the CIO took aim at a
host of lesser targets, including Cleveland's stove foundries.
Through March, April, and May of 1937, crowds gathered
to hear organizers call for unionization of the town's stove
industry. Executives, evidently sensing that the appeals had
not fallen entirely on deaf ears, granted two back-to-back
wage increases. Nonetheless, large numbers of workers, who
had been living on short rations since 1930, were growing
more militant, less amenable to conciliation. Another group
mistrusted unions, regarding them as synonymous with outside
interference. Sides formed, and families divided along pro-
union and anti-union lines. As tensions mounted, some of
Dixie's molders took to packing pistols in their toolboxes.
The controversy came to a head in late May, when groups
of employees at each of the foundries organized as units of
the CIO.

The battle lines had been drawn, and on June 11 the CIO
called a general strike at the foundries. At nine o'clock that
morning an employee of Dixie—witnesses later differed as
to his identity—sounded the steam whistle, signalling quitting
time. In response, 650 employees laid down their tools and

walked out. Some of them set up a picket line, which became the scene of skirmishes and vandalism. Because those remaining were too few to operate the plant, Dixie shut down, as did the town's other strike-bound stove companies.

The companies remained idle through June, with neither side showing a willingness to compromise. A break in the deadlock came during early July, when a group of strikers formed a back-to-work committee and, in meetings with Rymer and the head of another company, claimed that the majority of strikers were ready to return to work. According to several accounts, the strikers had become disillusioned by what they considered the CIO's failure to deliver on promises to see the men through with regular outlays of food. Whatever the cause, the CIO clearly lost control of its local members on July 10, when the molders voted to return to work at the same wages and under the same conditions prevailing before the strike. Moreover, they selected as their sole bargaining agent the IMU, which had not only refrained from supporting their strike but also was an affiliate of the AFL, an organization that had locked horns with the CIO.

Following the molders' action, Dixie Foundry reopened, on July 12, and the remainder of Cleveland's stove companies were up and running by the next day. Although diehard CIO pickets would maintain a lonely vigil outside Dixie's gates through the summer and into the winter, the main current of action had passed them by.

When the CIO faltered, the AFL jumped into the breach opened by its rival. Having earlier declared CIO activity needlessly disruptive, the IMU of the AFL turned around and declared strikes at Dixie on July 25 and again on the 28th. A protracted dispute ensued. Brad and LeRoy Rymer fired all striking workers, replacing them with others. Retaliating, the IMU put Dixie on the national list of companies whose products were to be boycotted. Next, a local court issued an injunction against picketing and, when the IMU failed to comply, police jailed the pickets. The IMU countered by filing with the National Labor Relations Board (NLRB) sixty-five complaints charging Dixie with unfair labor practices.

It was a time of bitter disappointment for Rymer. His own nephew by marriage, a Dixie employee, played a prominent role in the strike. And as the NLRB hearing progressed, Rymer felt himself victimized and powerless to set matters right. Although not given to dashing off letters to Washington, he wrote a U.S. Senator to complain at length about the treatment Dixie had received at the hands of the NLRB. "I do not have language to express my sentiments regarding the tactics of the labor board hearing," he began. "All the unfair tactics [were those of] the examiner who sat on the bench. . . . He would plead for my attorney not to ask certain questions. . . . They wanted 44 cents a page [for the transcript] . . . an exorbitant price . . . which is discriminatory beyond any doubt. . . . My way of seeing [it is that] there is only one side and that is absolutely the labor side and none other. . . . I want to say that I am for the fair and right thing between employer and labor . . . but we certainly need a housecleaning of the labor board."

On April 8, 1938, as the hearing neared a close, Rymer reluctantly agreed to sign a contract ending the dispute. By its principal terms, management recognized the IMU as a bargaining agent of Dixie's unionized employees only; agreed to rehire, with certain exceptions, IMU members terminated for taking part in the strike; and promised to furnish molders some additional supplies.

Not surprisingly, relations between the IMU and Dixie

remained strained. In particular, the mechanics of rehiring strikers proved to be a sore spot. Dixie's files bulged with correspondence on one disagreement or another. Typical of these was the union's contention that "cat skinners" were being given jobs in preference to strikers on the recall list. Responding to the charge, Dixie's attorney wrote the president of IMU Local 194: "As you know it has been the custom in this foundry and in all other foundries to work a few men who are extra men called 'cat skinners.' The cat skinners report to work every morning, and if any of the regular molders are not there for work, the cat skinners are given their floors for the day. The rule in all foundries is that whenever there is a vacancy, either by an old moulder quitting, or by new work added, the first floor goes to the first cat skinner, and, if needed, a new cat skinner is taken on. This is what the company has done."

Despite the disagreements, after almost a year industrial peace—if not harmony—had returned. But so had the depression. The economy, on the mend since mid-1933, suffered a relapse in late 1937. Unemployment climbed from fourteen percent back up to twenty percent, and the Dow Jones average fell sharply. Where Dixie had paid wages totalling $465,000 in 1937, it paid only $268,000 in 1938. Profits were also off, by more than thirty percent. The outlook improved somewhat in 1939, but not until the nation embarked on a military buildup in 1940 did the economy recover fully.

Dixie came out of the maelstrom of the thirties tested and tempered by adversity. It had survived a succession of lean years, a schism in top management, and protracted labor strife. Nor had the crises brought on a failure of nerve, a rigid caution easily mistaken for sound business policy. On the contrary, there was a new spirit of enterprise, sparked by an intense yet quiet young man who had joined the company in 1937 and who would exert profound influence on its destiny: S. Bradford Rymer, Jr. Although he had been named for his father, nobody called him Brad, and the S in front of the name still stood for nothing but S. To one and all he was known by a nickname, Skeet. He had acquired it as a toddler when a friend of the family, watching his quick movements, remarked: "Why, he's just like a skeeter."

His parents had seen in Skeet's early vigor and drive heralds of great promise. One day, when Skeet was nine months old, Brad had come home with a present, a tiny wooden stool, which he set before his son. As Clara Rymer recalled, Skeet picked up the stool and, taking his first steps, carried it across the room and placed it neatly beside his bed. Amazed and delighted, Brad declared, "Mother, there is our businessman."

A graduate of Georgia Tech, Skeet was Dixie's first engineer, but when he went to work he did nothing to call attention to that fact or to his ambitions for the company. Instead, he "hung around for a year or two in coveralls picking up scrap," as he described it. He also charged the cupola, a sweaty job which, veteran molders laughingly remembered, left him looking "like he'd been drug through the creek." He worked as a laborer in every department, grinding stove tops, mounting heaters, crating merchandise, and repairing returned goods. With typical thoroughness, he was doing his homework: watching closely, absorbing details, and forming ideas.

In 1939 he began to put his ideas into action, altering the way Dixie operated. Nothing better symbolized these changes than the motorized assembly line that he installed. It was the company's first, and with it Dixie took its first step into the age of mass production. During the next months he streamlined manufacturing processes throughout the plant, often over the protests of supervisors—who left in droves—but with the approval of his father. Tools and materials were placed so as to reduce the time workers spent locating them, parts were standardized, and sub-assembly stations were added to smooth out kinks in production.

By applying principles of industrial management in wide use since World War I, Skeet was gradually bringing efficiency and economy to what had been a job shop of stop-and-go production. Other projects were in the works, including Dixie's first line of engineered gas ranges. But these were interrupted on December 7, 1941, when a telex flashed across the Pacific: *Air Raid, Pearl Harbor—This Is No Drill.* For the next three years, Rymer's organizational talents were limited to instructing pilots for the Air Corp. During those years, Dixie would face the uncertainties of a world turned upside down by war.

5.

Moment of Reckoning

THE GREAT DEPRESSION became history when America shifted to a wartime footing in 1941. As military contracts poured out of Washington, industry experienced a boom unrivaled even during the glory days of the twenties. The automobile industry plunged into the manufacture of tanks, trucks, and weapons. All manner of new products and devices went into production: synthetic rubber, radar, proximity fuses, penicillin, DDT, and of course the atomic bomb. In the South alone, $3.8 billion was invested to expand plants during the war years.

Military contracts were highly lucrative, because manufacturers were asked to produce with little regard for economy or for anything else except quantity and speed. The windfall profits were, however, offset by an excess-profits tax and, in many cases, by the perils of converting back to peacetime production. After four years of making, say, shell casings or parachute flares, many small and medium-size companies lost touch with their old customers, grew complacent about costs, underestimated the expense of post-war retooling and, in consequence, never quite regained their former stature. Casualties among gas range manufacturers were particularly heavy: of the 269 companies going into the war, only 125 would be left in 1948.

Dixie Foundry escaped the potentially ruinous conversion

from plowshares to swords, thanks to a quirk of fate. Shortly after Pearl Harbor it seemed only a matter of weeks until Dixie would come under the control of the War Production Board, which Congress had created and invested with emergency powers to order companies to produce designated war goods or else shut down. Nearby Hardwick Stove, its assembly lines nationalized in 1942, would switch to the production of aircraft parts. But Dixie's failure to introduce the new line of engineered gas ranges in 1941 depressed annual sales below $2 million, which happened to be the minimum sales figure required by the Board before it conscripted a company.

As a further boon, the Board put Dixie on the list of small manufacturers designated to supply stoves to the country and the military. This designation allowed the company to go on making its basic products, but not without some big changes. For one thing, extensive modifications in design were required. Only the most Spartan models could be made, and whenever possible their components had to be fabricated of non-essential materials such as asbestos, which replaced much of the steel in side panels. These constraints sidetracked the program of design and engineering improvements begun in 1939.

Shortages of raw materials also posed a continual threat. At one point the government imposed a ten-pound limit on the purchase of nails, which Dixie's crating department used by the millions. To keep the department running, a stock clerk, Willard Corbit, often went from one hardware store to another, in Cleveland and out of town, buying ten pounds of nails at a time until he had accumulated several hundred pounds worth. And the scramble for raw materials often sent LeRoy Rymer to Washington in search of precious allocations from the War Production Board.

Despite the design restrictions and material shortages, Dixie could count on a limitless demand for its basic products, especially heaters, which wound up in military posts around the world. And the company could continue to fill orders, on a "limited quota basis," from its distributors and dealers, maintaining its link with the civilian marketplace. The eventual costs of retooling for peacetime, though not insignificant, would be minimal compared to those of many competitors drafted into the war effort.

Thus favored by events, the company proceeded to make money as never before. In 1943 it sold $3.6 million in merchandise, paid a whopping $751,000 in excess-profits tax, and still ended the year with a profit of $284,986. Despite the hefty earnings, dividends rose only slightly, for Brad Rymer had decided to retain large cash reserves against the possibility of a post-war slump. Having twice before been driven to the brink when booms collapsed, Rymer was taking no chances.

With earnings accumulating, free and clear of the expense of major retooling, Dixie was financially well off in comparison with previous years. Its position continued to improve when, instead of contracting, the economy raced ahead in 1945. Forecasts of the usual post-bellum recession had not taken into account the staggering rise in disposable income between 1939 and 1945, when the average weekly wage of industrial workers increased eighty-nine percent, while the cost of living went up only twenty-nine percent. Nor had the forecasters appreciated that consumer demand had reached seismic proportions. Bottled up first by depression and then by wartime rationing, consumer spending broke loose and rushed toward any available outlet. Goods were still scarce, which seemed to make that new car or refrigerator all the more desirable.

Cost and quality were of scant concern to people who for more than a decade had postponed all but essential purchases. Consumers went on a buying spree. In a single year, 1946, Dixie earned $697,036—a staggering sum, considering that it was just shy of total earnings for the entire decade of the thirties.

By 1946 Brad Rymer could look back with justifiable pride on what he had achieved at Dixie since its inception thirty years before. He had started a nickel-and-dime foundry and, against most expectations except his own, built it into a multi-million-dollar company. But unlike some self-made men who have beat the odds, he did not hold on to power after his ability to exercise it had diminished. When in 1944 he suffered a heart attack, he gradually transferred authority to his sons. He went so far as to tell them that they ought to begin considering which one of them should succeed him.

Although the sons worked as a team, each tended to specialize in certain aspects of the business. LeRoy, who alone among his brothers had remained at Dixie through the war and together with his father had guided the company through that difficult period, exercised control over day-to-day operations, with especial attention to purchasing. Marvin continued to direct the sales force, assisted by his brother Robert, who had joined the company in 1939, had since been named treasurer and credit manager, and was now concentrating on sales to one of those industries that sprang up after the war: mobile homes. Skeet, picking up where he had left off, set to modernizing the company.

Under Skeet's direction, Dixie embarked on a major expansion in 1945. One of the first additions to the plant was a

$30,000 Verson press, a 400-ton behemoth that stamped in one operation steel parts formerly fabricated in a series of presses operated by many workmen. Skeet knew that while brawn and native cunning had been key ingredients in Dixie's success, these could not always compensate for the company's lack of technical competence. With this in mind, Rymer recruited a professional engineer named Harold Moss. An Ohioan with a precise turn of mind, Moss had a direct manner and an accent that did not immediately endear him to all at Dixie. For his own part, he was none too impressed by what passed for engineering tolerances in 1946, later recalling that the company's measuring device was a yardstick and that "if parts fit together within an eighth of an inch, that was considered fine."

Perhaps few would have predicted at the time that he would go on to oversee nearly four decades of technological change at the company, design and build roughly two-thirds of its future additions, and in the process become something of an institution around the plant. The chances of that seemed slim to Moss himself during his first month there, when Rymer dropped in on him one day and said, "Harold, I want you to build an enameling plant." Taken aback, Moss protested, "Hell, Skeet, I've never even seen one." Unimpressed, Rymer replied, "You can learn, can't you?" Moss could and did.

Porcelain enamel, a variety of glass that at high temperatures fuses onto steel to seal out rust and form an attractive, impervious finish, had become a standard feature on stoves by the late twenties. Since then, Dixie's officers had periodically agreed that the construction of an enameling plant was a must. In its absence, the company bought all enameled parts at premium prices from two sources, one of which, the Cleveland Enamel Company, was a subsidiary of Dixie's competitor,

Hardwick Stove Company. This arrangement forced up manu-facturing costs, but with capital scarce through the thirties, the officers had put off investing appreciable sums in a plant.

The project took on new urgency in 1946, when steel shortages occurred nationwide. Scarcity, combined with fed-eral price controls, soon spawned a flourishing black market where steel commanded prices approaching those of semi-precious metals. This placed Dixie at risk, since it depended on outside suppliers for the steel as well as for the finishing of enameled parts. The extent of the danger became evident when Cleveland Enamel, moving to conserve its inventories of steel, declined to fill Dixie's orders for parts.

By this time, Harold Moss and an associate, Ed Yarbrough, were well along in the construction of the enameling plant, which opened in July of 1947. But the steel shortage continued to plague Dixie. Unable to purchase sufficient stock from mills, the Rymer brothers had no choice but to search out and purchase additional steel on the black market. LeRoy made frequent trips to Chicago, where with cash in one pocket and, on occasion, a pistol in the other, he dickered with profiteers in warehouses up and down the railroad yards. Harold Moss, a reluctant participant in one of these buying expedi-tions, recalled the time LeRoy summoned him to a hotel room in Chicago, threw $50,000 in bundled bills on the bed, and gave him the name and address of a man who was waiting in the railroad yards to sell a load of steel. The arrange-ments had been made, said LeRoy, and all that remained was for Moss to deliver the money. This was a bit more than Moss had bargained for when he came to Chicago to hire a draftsman. But not wishing to seem unappreciative of the high trust reposed in him, he carried out the mission—with slight modifications. Instead of going directly to the rendezvous, Moss first deposited the money in a bank, then met his man, watched the steel being loaded, and that done, invited the man to accompany him back to the bank in order to collect the money.

For all the expense, trouble, and danger involved in these dealings, Dixie often netted steel of the poorest quality. When nothing better was to be had, LeRoy or Skeet would buy ingots from antiquated mills that had been shut down years before but, like certain gold mines once deemed to be worked out, reopened after prices shot up. Before the ingots could be used, they had to be shipped to another mill and rolled into sheets there, at further expense. Compelled at times to buy stock sight unseen, the Rymers once ended up with a load of brittle, rusted steel salvaged from a shipwreck in the waters off the West Coast.

In the spring of 1948 the steel shortage paled in significance as a far more serious threat loomed at Dixie. Business dried up overnight. As Robert Rymer described it, "one morning we woke up and found there were no orders." Nothing quite like this sudden reversal had happened to the company since 1919, when Brad Rymer was caught with a mountain of sugar kettles and no customers.

The immediate cause lay outside the company. The public, sated after two years of record spending, had cut back on purchases, with the result that the pipelines between factories and stores were full to overflowing with unsold merchandise. A recession had begun, but it did not fully account for the fact that Dixie was performing as though rocked by a major depression. Sales, which had been running at about $450,000 a month for the past two years, plunged to $59,000 one month. Most of that amount came from an unexpected source—the mobile home industry—a promising but fledgling sideline that the officers had considered no more than a minor contributor to income. Yet, had Dixie been forced to rely on its supposedly established lines, then, according to Skeet Rymer, the plant "would not have been running" that month. Old segments of the business had collapsed, while a new one held firm. Something was wrong.

Instead of blaming the economy, Skeet looked at Dixie itself. He noted two disturbing trends. First, the volume of complaints against Dixie ranges had been increasing as fast as sales since 1945. Second, many of the independent distributors who acted as middlemen between the company and retailers had rechanneled their sales energies into other, more easily saleable, merchandise when the slump came. The recession, Rymer concluded, revealed internal weaknesses that had gone unnoticed in the rush to satisfy the enormous and largely indiscriminate appetite of consumers. Dixie had neither the merchandise nor the merchandisers to please buyers who were now in a finicky mood. As Rymer later explained: "Following World War II there was such a demand for all merchandise that it was a matter of obtaining the material and manufacturing the products, rather than doing an overall balanced job of making and selling quality products. When the tremendous decrease in sales occurred, it was realized that we did not have a product nor did we have a selling organization."

Either deficiency was extremely hazardous, and the two combined were potentially lethal. Management, in which Skeet exercised a decisive voice, decided to grapple first with the problem in manufacturing, reasoning that competitive, quality products were a prerequisite to building a new sales force. Besides taking the obvious measures—beefing up quality control and engineering—the officers also recognized that corporate means and ends were out of kilter. Dixie offered more products than it had the resources to manufacture and promote effectively. There were gas ranges to suit every taste and pocketbook, as well as an assortment of coal-and-wood-burning stoves and ranges. Dixie had a finger in many markets but a hold on none.

Overextended and outmaneuvered by competitors, the officers adopted a new strategy: to concentrate forces and direct them toward a target of opportunity. In place of the scattergun approach, Dixie would zero in on the market for low-to-medium priced gas ranges. Deluxe, pricey models were dropped, and in 1949 the company phased out coal-and-wood burners—dinosaurs that ate up resources and returned only a trickle of income. The freed-up resources went into a new line of gas ranges. Styled by Chicago designer Charles T. Waltman and engineered by Harold Moss, the line was introduced at the Chicago Furniture Market in 1949.

The improved line sold briskly, but its significance lay less in immediate paybacks than in the aboutface that it represented. In a business as competitive as stove making, it paid a company to know who it was and what it did well. The officers had shown the capacity to rethink time-honored assumptions. Now, instead of turning out a smorgasbord of products, many of which languished in inventory, Dixie was committed to building more quality and less cost into gas ranges designed specifically for the mass market. "It was from this basic line of ranges," Skeet Rymer remarked eighteen years later, "that the modern growth of [the company] today stems."

Indeed, Dixie had arrived at the end of its beginning. An era, a way of doing business, was passing. During that era the cooking-appliance industry had changed dramatically, from a hodgepodge of more than two thousand stove foundries to a core of fewer than two hundred gas- and electric-range manufacturers. In 1917, the Hanks Stove & Range Company was a thriving business when its founder, Jefferson Davis Hanks, assisted at the birth of Dixie Foundry. In 1949, Hanks's company was a walking corpse, still producing nothing but the potbellied stoves and wood-burning ranges that time had turned into museum pieces. It would fold in 1955. Brad Rymer, in contrast, had kept Dixie one jump ahead of obsolescence, gradually eliminating a string of outdated products —hollow ware, dog irons, sugar kettles—while phasing in gas ranges.

But another era had begun. In it, the Dixies of the industry— the small regional gas range makers—were losing ground to a few companies with the size, name brands, and sales muscle to capture national markets. Compared to the Tappans, Calorics, and American Stoves, Dixie was, according to Skeet Rymer, "insignificant in the gas range industry . . . a very small fish in a big pond of manufacturers producing and selling low-priced ranges." And in that pond the rewards were the lowest per-unit profits in the industry.

In order to compete for more than the leavings of others, management needed to retool for dynamic growth, creating a national sales force and a recognizable brand name. That would be a feat not unlike re-building the engine and driveshaft of a car in motion. Balance, timing, and the willingness to take risks were essential to the man at the wheel.

Brad Rymer had steered Dixie as far as he could go. At age seventy, largely incapacitated by chronic heart fibrillations, he decided to retire to the newly-created position of chairman of the board. On January 1, 1950, the mantle of leadership passed to Skeet Rymer. As president, Skeet took responsibility for a company whose finest hour was either past or yet to come, depending on his ability to venture beyond past successes and adapt to a new set of realities.

6.

Going Flat Out

FROM THE START of his presidency, Skeet Rymer, at age thirty-five, exercised authority on the strength of his own personality and performance. Although he was the son, namesake, and hand-picked successor of Dixie's founder, he scrupulously avoided the dynastic claim to leadership invoked with varying degrees of subtlety and success by many other scions of family enterprises. In ways large and small, Rymer let it be known that the presidency was not a hereditary title conferring privileges on its holder and his loyal retainers. So long as Rymer held the office, there would be no private dining rooms or reserved parking spaces—not for him or for anyone else. (The only exception was to maintain the parking spaces traditionally reserved for his father and brothers.) Trivial though that policy might appear, it conveyed an important message: everybody, from the president down, would have to find his place in the company each day.

To Rymer's credit and the company's lasting benefit, he encouraged a work ethic and the spirit of enterprise necessary for survival in a fiercely competitive industry. He approached his work with deadly seriousness, as if it were the very test of his existence. No one could help noticing that he was at the plant early and late, putting in seventy or eighty hours a week, every week. Some of his colleagues were aware, too, that he had given up golf and flying; hobbies were a luxury he no longer allowed himself. Asked later if he had ever regretted those years of self-imposed sacrifice, he replied: "If you don't do the pick-and-shovel work, you're not going to have any glamour to enjoy."

A company born to greatness was a concept as alien to Rymer's thinking as it was to Dixie's situation. There was much spadework to be done before Dixie could lay claim to importance.

Rymer's strategy in the early 1950s was less remarkable for its novelty than for the fact that it was being put into action. According to the results of a study conducted in 1952 by the consulting firm of Stevenson, Jordan & Harrison: "In the [late] 1940s management decided to become a major factor in the production of gas ranges. This in itself was not momentous. Probably most of the other companies in the industry had made the same decision, not once, but many times. The momentous part of the Dixie decision was that it evolved into a well conceived plan of concrete action."

The consultants went on to report that the initial phase of this plan had been completed, that manufacturing and design had been overhauled so as to yield gas ranges with sales appeal in the mass market. These improvements, if kept current, were the price of admission to the next phase, which called for a drastic change in sales approach. The company had always sold its wares through a network of distributors, independent brokers who called on dealers as representatives of several companies including makers of gas ranges, refrigerators, radios and hi-fis. By using these middlemen, Dixie saved the cost of starting its own sales force but lost the slice of profits that went to the distributor. In the long run it was a false economy, particularly since other companies were switching to salesmen and thereby seizing a pricing advantage over

Dixie. Moreover, brokered business had other drawbacks. It was unpredictable, subject to sharp drops like the one in 1949. And in granting exclusive franchises to distributors, the company forfeited its right to develop factory-trained salesmen dedicated solely to promoting its products; if a distributor chose to push goods other than Dixie's, there was not much the company could do about it. The system defied control.

A sales force, on the other hand, could be held accountable for executing a systematic marketing plan. And by selling directly to dealers, the salesman would eliminate the distributor's slice of profits and place Dixie in closer contact with dealers and the marketplace.

So critical was the need for a sales force that Rymer intended to develop one in the short span of ten years. Time was of the essence, for, as Rymer sized up matters in 1952, Dixie had perhaps a decade in which to emerge as a "major factor in the production of gas ranges." By his definition, this meant boosting the company's share of total gas range sales from barely three percent to ten percent by 1962. If that came to pass, then Dixie would, the consultants projected, "probably be the largest manufacturer in the industry—certainly larger than any manufacturer now is." The likelihood of that happening was another question, and one that the consultants approached diplomatically, with guarded language. Under the heading "Growth May Be Difficult," they noted: "This schedule is optimistic to the point that it leaves no margin for error or omission. Since many of [Dixie's] competitors have demonstrated their ability as sales strategists it is apparent that Dixie sales methods must come close to perfection if the goal is to be reached."

If the goal strained even the determined optimism of consultants, the plan was nonetheless grounded in reality. Before long there would be two classes of gas range makers: those that had grown on a grand scale and those that were no longer around.

Size had not always mattered in the industry, which from its inception had been composed primarily of small regional manufacturers, such as Dixie. During the twenties a few companies grew larger and advertised nationally, but these did not encroach on their smaller competitors. There had been business enough for all. It was a congenial field for the industrialist of small means—altogether different from the electric range industry, where giants such as General Electric, Westinghouse, and Frigidaire held sway.

But like corner groceries and Chinese laundries, the small regionals were an endangered species in 1952. Electric ranges, benefiting from drastic improvements in technology and efficiency, were surging in popularity, cutting deep inroads into the gas range industry. In 1946 gas ranges outsold electrics three-to-one, but by 1959 sales would be almost even and the balance would tip in favor of electrics during the 1960s.

Gas range makers were up against formidable opponents. The General Electrics and Westinghouses brought a new weapon to the battlefield: national advertising and marketing on a massive scale. These promotional blitzes did what, in the terminology of the industry, is known as "pre-selling"— predisposing many customers to buy a name brand irrespective of how it compared to less recognizable brands. As multi-million-dollar promotions induced demand for a few labels, many widely respected names—Detroit Jewel, Estate, O'Keefe & Merritt, Universal—were fading into obscurity, eventually to die or become the property of others. And newcomers to the business achieved consistent results: of the two companies entering the field after World War II, both withdrew before 1957.

The economics of remaining small looked impossible to Rymer. One alternative was to marry size, even at the cost of independence. He had talked with executives of Tappan about a merger, but, as he informed Dixie's board in October of 1952, the discussions had produced "no area for agreement or further negotiation." Still, his pick-and-shovel work at Dixie went on.

In 1952 Marvin Rymer, working closely with Skeet, assembled the nucleus of a sales force, which would grow to sixty-seven men by 1959 and include stellar performers such as Harold Logan, Lonnie Burchett, Fritz Deininger, Joe Davis, Ernest Fielden, William Sharpe, Henry Hackney, Euel Burche, Jack Gillespie, and Barney Millican. The Rymers emphasized results rather than regimentation in sales, a style of management that, then and later, was a distinctive feature of the company. A consultant's evaluation of salesman Sharpe warned: "Do not send a new man out with Sharpe. His methods are highly effective for Sharpe, but might get a neophyte thrown out of the store." The reputation for unorthodoxy could have landed Sharpe in the corporate penalty box. But performance outweighed conformance at Dixie, and the maverick Sharpe went on to a successful career there.

The salesforce had its work cut out for it: to take Dixie into thousands of retail outlets nationwide, primarily appliance dealers, hardwares, and furniture stores. Their task was complicated by the fact that many retailers and most consumers had never heard of Dixie. The Dixie salesman, unlike his opposite number at larger companies, seldom enjoyed the advantage of preaching to the converted. So that his message would not fall entirely on deaf ears, management underwrote

Dixie's first foray into the mass media. Though modest, the debut was made before a national audience. During 1953 the company advertised its ranges in seven popular magazines catering to housewives: *Better Homes & Gardens, Family Circle, Everywoman's, Woman's Day, Holland's, Sunset,* and *What's New In Home Economics.* Lack of funds barred access to the hot new conduit of advertising, television, which held America spellbound, even causing many households to give up the family dinner for the TV dinner.

The initiatives taken in national sales and advertising were followed by a notable addition to products when, in 1954, the assembly lines at Dixie began to turn out electric ranges. The action won mixed reviews from gas utilities and from the Gas Appliance Manufacturers Association, which were trying to circle the wagons. But Rymer's thinking on the subject went beyond the partisan stance of the gas industry. There was no turning back the clock to the time when gas was the fuel of choice in three out of every four kitchens. Electrics would play an integral part in the cooking appliance industry taking shape. And while Rymer rated Dixie's immediate opportunities in electrics as slim, he intended to move onto the path of growth that the industry had taken.

Rymer was also adding appreciably to the store of talent and influence at Dixie's disposal. By 1955 he had won a few powerful converts to his vision for the company. The first of these was the forty-three-year-old president of Atlanta's Citizens & Southern National Bank, Mills B. Lane, Jr. A go-go banker in the era of go-slow banking, Lane raised eyebrows among his straitlaced colleagues. "Flamboyant," "offbeat," "freewheeling," and "zany" were some of the milder adjectives applied to him, and with considerable accuracy. He once rolled into an officers' meeting at the wheel of a toy sportscar, his way of dramatizing the need for speedy decisions. He customarily answered his telephone with a booming "It's a wonderful world!" and wore ties emblazoned with the same message. "Can I sell you some money today?" he greeted customers. Despite charges of defiling the temple of Morgan with the hype of Barnum, Lane possessed several qualities that a small industrialist with big ambitions could appreciate. Among them were unquenchable optimism, the audacity to bankroll schemes others rejected as unsound, and the willingness to listen to a loan proposal and say yes or no on the spot. Lane and Rymer took to each other immediately, though they could not have been more different in personal styles. Decades later, after Lane's record at C&S had come under attack, Rymer still remembered his friend's generosity of spirit: "Mills would bet on people. He trusted people, and if he believed in you he would do whatever was necessary to see you through."

Lane served as Dixie's banker, financial advisor, and, later, one of its directors. More important, though, he helped Rymer make valuable connections in the business world outside Cleveland and the usual trade associations. In matchmaking, he showed particular acuteness, seeming to know precisely the sort of person who would hit it off with Dixie's president. In 1950 he introduced Rymer to Francis Shackelford, a partner in the Atlanta law firm of Alston, Miller & Gaines. Although Shackleford had collected diplomas from the Lawrenceville School, Princeton University, and Harvard Law School, he downplayed his Ivy League background. He was a hard-driving pragmatist, a lawyer impatient with legal shawdowboxing— a man after Rymer's own heart. He became not only Dixie's legal counsel but also, in 1955, the first director since Grover Brown to come from outside the Rymer family.

It was also through Mills Lane that Rymer gained admission to the Young Presidents Organization (YPO). Formed in 1950 by Ray Hickock, president of Hickock Belt Company, the YPO limited its membership to the early-blooming executive who, by age thirty-nine, had become head of a company doing three million dollars in sales, or in the case of a financial institution, having fifty million dollars in assets. At YPO conventions Rymer met kindred spirits, gaining from them insight as well as the conviction that to aim high was not necessarily to tilt at windmills. He formed friendships with some of the nation's best and brightest businessmen, including Kemmons Wilson, founder of Holiday Inns; Winton (Red) Blount, president of Blount Construction and later Postmaster General during the Nixon Administration; Dillard Munford, president of Munford, Inc.; and Bo Callaway, president of Callaway Gardens and Secretary of the Army during the Ford Administration. And Rymer was getting to know two men who would figure directly in Dixie's future: Willard F. (Al) Rockwell, Jr., founder and CEO of Rockwell International; and John Marks Templeton, a multimillionaire investor whom *Forbes* would hail "a great genius . . . one of a handful of true investment greats in a field crowded with mediocrity and bloated reputations." Looking back on his experience in the YPO, Rymer said, "after my family, religion, and work, it was the most influential activity in my life."

Nineteen fifty-seven was a year for breaking ground in unfamiliar territory. On May 28, Dixie's board voted to form not one but two subsidiaries. Both were long shots, and one bore a name that did not roll easily off the tongues of most directors. It was Cocinas Dixie De Venezuela. Headquartered

in Caracas, Cocinas Dixie traced its origin back to a meeting
that Francis Shackelford had arranged between Skeet Rymer
and an Atlantan by the name of A. D. (Dick) Adair, Jr. A
graduate of Princeton, a lawyer by training but not by practice,
Adair was tall and ruggedly charming and he carried himself
in a way that said this man is equally capable of holding his
own in a Mayfair drawing room or a Karachi opium den.
Adair had spent several years managing his family's fertilizer
business, but now he was looking for work that would take
him abroad. Rymer hired him to scout out opportunities for
manufacturing Dixie ranges in South America, where a burgeoning population of potential consumers, cheap labor, and
a supposedly pro-business climate were attracting droves of
American manufacturers.

As Dixie's emissary to South America, Adair was accompa-
nied by his wife, Virginia, a woman of unfailing charm with
a knack for moving confidently in foreign parts. While others
might have considered South America a hardship posting,
she viewed it as an adventure. The Adairs were a formidable
diplomatic team, engaging, energetic, able to spot and cultivate valuable contacts.

Within a year, Adair's reconnoitering led to the formation
of Cocinas Dixie. Under Adair's direction the subsidiary would
contract for the assembly of ranges from Valencia's Industrias
Integradas S.A., a Rockefeller-financed experiment in Vene-
zuelan development that manufactured to order for such companies as Bendix, Hupp, Sunray Stove, Tyler Refrigeration,
and Monroe Auto Equipment. Dixie ranges produced by Industrias Integradas would then be sold throughout Venezuela.
And in time, with luck, Cocinas Dixie would extend its manufacturing and sales into Argentina, Peru, and Brazil.

The second subsidiary formed in May of 1957 was called

Dixie-Narco. Like the South American venture, it existed to explore for new sources of income, this time in the field of vending machines. That possibility had been suggested to Rymer by the man who became the minority owner of Dixie-Narco, Chattanooga businessman Carl Albert Navarre. Once a rising star in the Coca-Cola bottling empire of George Hunter, Navarre had struck out on his own after Hunter died and left most of the empire's assets to philanthropy. In 1957 Navarre was preparing to acquire a string of Coca-Cola bottling companies that would eventually stretch from St. Louis to Miami and abroad to Israel. The idea had occurred to him that dealing in soft-drink vending machines would make a natural sideline, and he had already created a small sales organization, called Narco, for that purpose. Narco represented a manufacturer that, Navarre learned, could be had at a good price: Victor Products, located nine miles west of Harpers Ferry, West Virginia, in the town of Ranson. With Victor, Navarre could expand from sales into manufacturing, but he lacked both the technical background and the inclination to go into manufacturing. That was where Rymer and Dixie came in. If Dixie would put up eighty-five percent of the capital and supply the vending machines, Navarre would supply their sales outlets in the Coca-Cola bottling industry. The alliance made sense to Rymer. In the early summer of 1957 Dixie-Narco purchased the Victor plant for $650,000, and with that Dixie stepped into a business that would prove no less contentious than the cooking appliance industry.

Both subsidiaries were risky investments, but management had earned the right to place a couple of small bets. Since 1949, Dixie's sales had tripled and then held steady, rising from $4.04 million to $12.9 million. Assets, too, had multiplied exponentially, from $2.84 million to $6.7 million. And profits consistently exceeded $500,000, even though during 1956 and 1957 management had pumped $1.5 million into expansions of the Cleveland plant, which now employed just over seven hundred persons. As a result of those gains, the company had, in seven years' time, risen from the bottom to the middle ranks of the gas range industry.

The progress was extraordinary, measured by almost any standard other than the one Rymer had applied. His timetable called for Dixie to reach the top of the industry by 1962, to capture ten percent of gas range sales by then. But the way up was heavily guarded, and Dixie was flying an unknown flag. As Rymer explained, "Dixie was not a popular brand name, except for paper cups." It was Brand X, and advertising was teaching consumers not to be fooled by Brand X. There was no substitute for a trademark that commanded recognition. For years Rymer had been searching for a brand name with sales appeal, and in the late summer of 1958 he was pretty sure that he had finally found it.

The brand, and the company that went with it, had several features that commended it to Rymer's attention. It had sold more gas ranges at retail than any other manufacturer. It numbered among its devoted customers such notables as Senator and Mrs. John F. Kennedy, Jane Fonda, and Marlon Brando. And its name had a nice ring: Magic Chef.

Like most gas range makers, Magic Chef had started out on a shoestring. On September 15, 1881, as President James Garfield lay dying of an assassin's bullet, two German immigrants, the brothers Louis and Charles Stockstrom, began to make stoves in a 25-by-45-foot workshop off their house in St. Louis. These stoves, which they called Quick Meals, burned gasoline, a byproduct of oil refineries that nobody other than stove makers saw much use for at the time.

Twenty years passed while the Stockstroms tinkered with their Quick Meals and put together small deals. Then the brothers hit it big. On Christmas eve, 1901, they incorporated the American Stove Company and, seven days into the new year, snapped up nine stove companies to form one of the largest companies of its kind in the nation.

But scarcely had American Stove taken hold when lightening struck. Oil refiners had discovered a way to coin money with gasoline. By altering its specific gravity, they could sell it at premium prices to the burgeoning automobile industry. The refiners' gain was the stove makers' loss, for the specific gravity that worked so well in the internal combustion engine did not work at all in the gasoline vapor stove. As automobiles and filling stations blanketed America, vapor stoves went the way of horseshoes and blacksmiths.

American Stove rebounded as a maker of ranges burning natural and manufactured gas, and in 1915 introduced a device that assured it a permanent place in the annals of cooking: the first thermostatically controlled range oven. The range featured a control knob, dubbed the Lorain Red Wheel after its color and place of manufacture (Lorain, Ohio), which took much of the guesswork and drudgery out of cooking. To master a range not equipped with temperature controls demanded vigilance and was largely a matter of burn and learn. But with the Red Wheel, a conscientious novice could cook meals to a turn without hovering over the stove.

American Stove had built the proverbial mousetrap, but the world did not beat a path to its door. Housewives viewed the Red Wheel as an expensive gimmick. The company found ways to soften their resistance, however. The original Red

Wheel had been marked off in degrees Fahrenheit but, since temperature settings were meaningless to cooks, the company replaced it with one on which the settings, though still calibrated to exact temperatures, now were labelled with terms out of the cook's traditional vocabulary: "Very Slow," "Slow," "Moderate," "Hot," "Quick," and "Very Hot." And the company published scores of cookbooks containing instructions for preparing meals on the Red Wheel stove.

By the mid-twenties the Red Wheel had caught on, and American Stove was growing apace, building new plants in Ohio and Indiana. It was also about this time that the executives began to look enviously at what Alfred Sloan of General Motors was doing for the automobile industry. While Ford sold only transportation, General Motors sold that and prestige, too. By slapping new chrome and curves on the same chassis every year, Sloan was encouraging car buyers to step on the fashion treadmill and trade in that old but serviceable model for the latest statement in upward social mobility.

If General Motors could engineer psychological obsolesence into cars, then, reasoned American Stove's executives, they would do the same with ranges. So they built the Cadillac of their industry. When it was ready to be unveiled, they arranged for the company's newsletter to beat a prolonged drumroll. The editors, in their lead article of August 1929, asked: "With all the improvements that the modern range possesses, including the oven heat regulator, to the modern woman it may still be a gas range, a little whiter, perhaps, than her mother's stove, but a gas range, nevertheless. Who will be the Moses to lead the tribes of gas range retailers out of the wilderness of cut rate prices, low quality, commonplace design, hideous clashing colors that harmonize with nothing, into the land of pre-sold goods—merchandise that people want, such as radios, iceless refrigerators, automobiles, and the like?"

Two months later the executives came down from Mount Sinai with a line of ranges they called Magic Chef. It had been styled not by an industrial designer but by Frank Alvah Parsons, director of the New York School of Fine Art. Sleek, resplendent, enamelled in rich colors, it looked more like a lacquered cabinet than like a stove. Two models, *Patrician* and *Jonquil,* sold for the astronomical price of $195. A lavish advertising campaign proclaimed Magic Chef the "New Vogue in Cooking," and featured stunning graphics that could have done justice to a Sotheby's prospectus.

Then the Great Depression forced cutbacks in 1933: the company said goodbye to *Patrician* and *Jonquil* and hello to black-and-white advertisements. But by that time Magic Chef had become a watchword for quality and high fashion, and by 1939 American Stove claimed to be selling forty-eight percent of the nation's gas ranges. It was the company's last hurrah.

After World War II American Stove plunged into a long free fall. Unable to convert successfully to peacetime production, its sales dipped from the $18.5 million of 1941 to $15.9 million in 1953. By then, the company had re-named itself Magic Chef, after its most famous product. But the name no longer worked magic for the company. As sales continued spiralling downward, the board allowed Arthur Stockstrom, son of Louis and CEO since 1938, to step aside to make room for a new man, Cecil M. Dunn. Lately president of the Estate Division of RCA, Dunn announced in a letter to salesmen that he had accepted the challenge to "regain Magic Chef's former enviable position." Some employees, however, eventually began to suspect that the liquidator had arrived.

Dunn gradually sold off most of the company's tangible assets: factories in St. Louis, Lorain, and Indianapolis; warehouses in Illinois; and corporate headquarters in St. Louis. Sales rose to $23 million in 1954, but the company posted a crippling loss of $4.28 million. In October of 1955 Dunn bought a small factory, Dortch Stove Works, located eighteen miles south of Nashville in Franklin, Tennessee. There he transferred what remained of Magic Chef.

Two years and a lot of red ink later, Dunn merged the company into Food Giant Markets, a chain of supermarkets located in California and owned by Wall Street financier Harold L. Fierman. But the only consequence of this move, so far as Magic Chef's employees could ever see, was that Food Giant summarily cancelled retirement programs and benefits.

The end was near in 1958. Sales had amounted to only $5.2 million by September, when Skeet Rymer telephoned Dunn and asked him if he was ready to sell. It so happened, Dunn said, that next week he would be passing through Cleveland on his way to Gatlinburg, Tennessee, where he planned to do a little fishing. He would stop off for a visit.

To all appearances, about the only asset left at Magic Chef was a name, soiled and headed for ruin but, according to a study made by the New York firm of D'Arcy Advertising, "still virtually a household word, having enjoyed a dominant position in the . . . past." The public's perception of Magic Chef lagged years behind reality; despite all, there yet remained some magic in the name. Dunn and Rymer came to terms quickly, and on October 1, Dixie bought Magic Chef for one million dollars. Rymer had caught a falling star.

7.

"At the Crossroads"

THE ACQUISITION of Magic Chef put Dixie on the high road to growth. Before the purchase, Dixie had been stuck in the sweatshop of private labelers, selling mostly no-name ranges at discounts to the buying cartels of large department stores that affixed their own labels and markups. In the appliance industry's garment district, pricing could make or break a company, as could the decisions of one or two buyers. And there was, said Skeet Rymer, another cause for worry: "We were saddled with the private labelers, and if they get into trouble, you are in trouble, too. We had too many eggs in one basket."

The Magic Chef brand name would allow Dixie not only to break its dependence on private labeling but also to step out on its own as a contender in the arena of medium-to-premium-priced ranges. Opportunity beckoned, and so did the hazards of seizing it. Specifically, there was the problem of marrying two dissimilar organizations, one a racehorse on its last legs, the other a workhorse in harness. But more was involved than a corporate re-shuffling and the drawing of a new organizational chart in which all the lines connected at the right places. The central question was that of corporate identity. Would the marriage's offspring be the spitting image of Dixie, of Magic Chef, or something different from either?

Before Dixie's board of directors squarely faced that question, they suffered a grievous loss when, on April 13, 1959, Brad Rymer died quietly in his sleep. In his later years, when Rymer would reminisce about Dixie, he had always taken pride in stating the fact that there "was never but twenty thousand dollars put into that business." At his death, the equity of that business stood at $6.8 million. Investors and their capital had played no part in Dixie's success. Out of grit and horsesense, Rymer had built a multi-million-dollar enterprise.

Brad Rymer had lived the American Dream, going from Greasey Creek to riches. But to the end, he never forgot that he was the young man who in 1904 had stepped off the train in Cleveland with ten dollars and change in his pocket. One could still recognize that man in the Cleveland *Daily Banner*'s tribute to Rymer, which read in part: "S. B. Rymer, known to thousands as 'Brad,' . . . never lost the common touch. . . . We have seen him many times hail a friend in overalls and talk to him on the street. . . . As a devout churchman, a farmer, a working man, a parent, a businessman, and a philanthropist, he touched many people. Those people are richer for that contact."

Taking Rymer's place as chairman of the board was his eldest son, LeRoy. In addition to LeRoy and Skeet, Dixie's board was composed of Marvin Rymer, vice-president of sales; Robert Rymer, secretary and treasurer; Brad's widow Clara; the Rymer sisters, Zola Graf, Ruth Dethero, and Roberta Keyes; and the single outsider, Francis Shackelford. They had decided to operate Dixie and Magic Chef as two separate organizations, each with its own plant, sales force, and brand name. Dixie would stand pat in the low-end of the market, leaving the middle and upper reaches to Magic Chef.

Selected to take charge of Magic Chef's sales was H. L. (Ike) Dethero, who had overseen Dixie's builder division and would go on to become a popular, three-term mayor of Cleveland. To supervise production at the Franklin plant, management tapped a Dixie veteran, David Griffith. All the pieces were in place, but some officers within the company did not view the new setup as necessarily final and permanent. Even as resources were being realigned, Skeet Rymer had confided to Shackelford, "If we can't run them separately, then we can certainly put them together."

The dual operations, as soon became evident, had drawbacks. Overhead rose and administrative snarls occurred as management coped with what were essentially needless duplications in staffs, advertising campaigns, product lines, and sales forces. Salesmen from the two entities often ended up slugging it out with one another rather than with their competitors. And the plant in Franklin, Tennessee, was being outfitted with new dies, which were for the most part similar to those at Cleveland and, in many cases, redundant.

Operating the two organizations as separate and distinct entitites had generated inefficiencies and friction, suggesting that the arrangement was unstable. Perhaps the companies would be stronger together than apart, for the weak point of each was the strong point of the other. Magic Chef had a name but not much of a product, while Dixie had a product but no name outside trade circles.

At the board meeting held on February 29, 1960, Skeet Rymer recommended that the two companies be combined into one which would operate under the name Magic Chef and throw its full weight behind that brand name. The directors, after some discussion, agreed to consider the proposal further before taking any action. When they assembled again, on May 30, Skeet argued vigorously for consolidation. While conceding that it would cause "many dislocations," he pointed out that the company stood to save "as much as one million dollars" by eliminating redundancies. He did not, however, rest his case on that one million dollars. "My opinion after sixteen months of operating Dixie and Magic Chef," he said, "is that potential volume and profits are much greater operating as one under Magic Chef than operating as two separate organizations." The choice was between the promise of the future and the pull of the past.

Rymer told the directors that in deciding the issue they would be determining the company's destiny. "We are standing at the crossroads today," he told them. "We can be a supplier of ranges to the world. Or we can enjoy a small comfortable business—maybe. We can go forward, or we can go backward. But we cannot stand still."

When everybody had had his say, at the end of one of the lengthiest board meetings in Dixie's history, the directors voted to put the two companies together, effective January 1, 1961. As a prelude to consolidation, the directors on December 6, 1960, adopted a new corporate identity, retiring the name Dixie for the one by which the company would become known to the world: Magic Chef, Inc.

Along with the new name came a memorable logo, dreamed up in 1939 by the advertising department of American Stove. It was, wrote its creator, a "comical figure, typically Walt Disney—a little chef in formal attire, like a headwaiter, but with a chef's cap." Over years of use, the little chef had developed a distinctive personality, claimed its creator, who wrote: "Sometimes [an advertising department] adopts a character as a symbol, [only] to become heartily sick of it in the passing of time. This is due to fixed rigidity, the inability of the character to adapt to changes of pace. [But] our little Magic Chef has kept fluid. It is a nimble little creature that is [as] ready for change . . . [as] a chameleon. He carries banners . . . or wields pointers . . . or does whatever will fit into the spirit of the program. He even multiplies himself into whole battalions of little chefs." Unpretentious, adaptable, protean, the little chef would prove a fitting standard bearer for Magic Chef, Inc.

On the eve of consolidation, in early 1961, the company reached a ten-year goal that had looked impossibly distant when set in 1952: to capture ten percent of the nation's gas range sales. For two straight years, about one out of every ten buyers of new ranges had chosen Magic Chef. By snaring ten percent of the market in less than a decade, the company had outstripped most of its old competitors, including next-door rival Hardwick Stove. While Hardwick outsold Dixie two-to-one in 1952, the ratio had turned the other way and would grow increasingly lopsided. Zooming sales, combined with the acquisition of Magic Chef, had transformed the "very small fish in a big pond" into one of the nation's four largest makers of gas ranges, on a par with Tappan, Caloric, Roper, and the Kenmore division of Sears, Roebuck.

Thus the company was in strong condition when it went under the knife of reorganization. The first cut—folding up the plant in Franklin—revealed how good a deal had been struck in the purchase of Magic Chef. After all the plant's equipment and fixtures had been culled and the desirable pieces removed to Cleveland, an appreciable surplus remained. It was put up for auction on Tuesday, September 26, 1961. Starting early that morning, the gavel banged down on assorted industrial machines, many of which weighed more than box-cars: suspension presses, double crank presses, hydraulic grinders and shapers, spot welders, air compressors, engine lathes, horizontal spindle drills, shearing squares, chain-driven overhead conveyors, drill presses, and a 250-ton Verson press brake. When the final bidding ended and the receipts were tallied, the day's take amounted to just under one million dollars—or slightly less than Cecil Dunn's selling price.

Rymer had bought a sleeping beauty. But he was not in the business of acquiring undervalued companies, stripping them of assets, then slipping off into the night. The money raised at auction, and considerably more, went into the reorganization, which called for expensive and disruptive changes: fusing two staffs and sales forces, rehabilitating Magic Chef's upper-priced line, moving out of private labeling, and accomplishing all this without losing hold of the business. When it became clear that expenses would overshoot initial estimates, Rymer stayed up one night preparing a request for a $2–4 million extension of the company's line of credit. At a meeting with Mills Lane the next day, Rymer launched into his carefully rehearsed presentation but had scarcely got beyond the prologue when Lane cut him short. "Skeet," said Lane, "I started out with you and I'll see you through to the end."

The new credit from C&S helped Magic Chef to expand despite a slump in sales and profits caused by the trauma of reorganization. Three quarters of a million went into new tooling, and taking form on the drawing board were one million dollars worth of additions to the plant, which, when completed in 1964, added 100,000 square feet of space and raised manufacturing capacity by sixty percent, to 1,700 ranges a day. With these and other expenditures, Rymer was putting the plant in shape to bear a far heavier load of production—$30 to $40 million annually.

As manufacturing power went up, Rymer took a hard look at the loadbearing capacity of the sales organization. It was, he concluded, designed to handle a lower volume of business than what was now contemplated. The potential for overload existed if he connected stepped-up production with the sales organization in place. To do so would be equivalent to plugging a one-hundred watt amplifier into a transitor radio; financial circuits might blow if unsold output backed up in the warehouses.

Skeet and his brother Marvin, head of sales, talked over the situation, agreeing that merchandising efforts lacked certain ingredients. One was a greater emphasis on promoting top-priced models, where the company's market was less developed but the profits greater than at the lower-priced end. Another was an intensive program to increase the number of salesmen and to train them in the mechanical workings of the Magic Chef range, thereby adding to their sales presentation an intimate knowledge of their products. Still another was to adopt somewhat more sophisticated marketing policies embracing such demographic and economic indicators as census figures, housing starts, buying power indices, and the like. Overall, Skeet wanted to crank up sales efforts, keeping the pressure on at all times.

Marvin, while appreciating the logic of this, came from a different school. During the 1930s, Marvin had resuscitated a moribund sales organization and run it with considerable success over the years, using a formula based primarily on good humor and hard bargaining. A virtuoso of person-to-person selling, he also possessed a gift for motivating salesmen. But by background and temperament, he felt most comfortable in a small, loosely structured business where he could set his own hours and be his own boss. In fact, he was engaged in starting a new business at the time. With the proposed change in sales, his position would develop into a more consuming job with diminished freedom of action. Understandably, he preferred not to be chained to the company as Skeet was. For that reason, Marvin resigned from management in January of 1962, forming his own business, a furniture factory, which grew and prospered.

Retaining the firm of Booz Allen as consultants, Skeet Rymer searched for a new sales manager. He was looking for a go-getter who had honed his marketing skills at companies much larger than Magic Chef, and he found the man in Roy Musselwhite. Lately product manager for the Norge Division of Borg-Warner, Musselwhite had earlier served as General Electric's national sales manager for water heaters. He brought to Magic Chef a high voltage personality—"the best pitch man I've ever seen," said one salesman of Musselwhite—and a wealth of experience in national marketing.

Among his first accomplishments was a training program in which new salesmen spent two months learning about the products they would sell. More was involved than plant tours, handouts, and lectures. Assigned a set of tools and a pair of overalls, the novice salesman spent hours on the shop floor, dirtying his hands while learning to fix defective ranges. In time the program expanded to include people at all levels, with everyone from Skeet Rymer to regional salesmen spending one week a year in the test kitchens.

According to the *Wall Street Journal*, this training exemplified Magic Chef's "know-your-product philosophy," which the *Journal*'s editors considered sufficiently unusual to take note of it in an article in 1977. "The emphasis placed on product training—almost to the point of saturation," Musselwhite told a group of analysts, "is one of the unique aspects of our program."

To Musselwhite also belongs a good part of the credit for Magic Chef's performance during the 1960s. While sales in the appliance industry as a whole grew by twenty-four percent, Magic Chef posted gains of 107 percent.

In 1963, Musselwhite arrived at a company that, even in the midst of internal reordering, was branching outward. In October, Rymer bought the Los Angeles-based Pan Pacific Manufacturing Company, which made small bottled-gas stoves for recreational vehicles (RVs). The transaction could not have come at a better time, for the RV business as well as the mobile home industry had begun to boom, and none of the major appliance makers—GE, Westinghouse, or the like—showed any inclination to supply its needs. Over the next decade, the industry would grow by twenty percent annually, and by 1971 the mobile home-RV division of Magic Chef, headed by Robert Rymer, would be selling thirty-five percent of all ranges placed in America's houses on wheels. Its share of sales to the RV industry would be even more impressive: seventy percent. By then, no other manufacturer would be in a position to challenge Magic Chef's dominance in sales to the RV industry. And in outfitting mobile homes, only Tappan would command a comparable chunk of sales. By making the right product at the right time, Magic Chef was stealing a march on its larger competitors.

The outlook for Magic Chef's other two subsidiaries was less promising. Dixie-Narco had posted losses of $125,000 during its first twenty-five months in business. Given the poor showing, Magic Chef's board had authorized Rymer to "explore the possibility" of disposing of the West Virginia subsidiary, but nothing came of it.

And on the international scene, the company's ambassador,

Dick Adair, had his share of troubles. Cocinas Dixie had turned a profit of $100,000 in 1960, but that year business conditions in Venezuela soured. As the country's economy unravelled, President Romulo Betancourt had clamped down on foreign exchange. Financial panic ensued, and there was open talk of insurrection. "The situation here is not good at all," Adair reported to Rymer on November 16. His letter described a country on the verge of chaos: "The banks are not selling any exchange. There is a black market (legal) which is now quoting 4.60 Bs [Bolivars] per Dollar. We raised our prices today 20 percent and I am sure it will completely stop all sales for a few days or even weeks but then things should settle down or get worse. . . . There are rumors of a scheduled takeover by the communists. . . . I think the good business cycle of Venezuela is completely finished and I only hope we can keep operating at a small profit."

Although Cocinas Dixie scratched out profits for a few years more, the bloom was off South America. Henceforth, Adair focused his efforts on a new front, Europe. It appeared to be ripe for development, especially since the Common Market (later the European Economic Community) had under-taken to lift tariff barriers and promote trade among its member nations. If European arteries of commerce were about to start gushing, then Magic Chef would be on the scene. Adair's survey of the continent eventually led him to Madrid, where late in 1962 he joined with a Spanish manufacturer, Jaime Olazabel, who agreed to go equal partners in a subsidiary incorporated by Adair, Magic Chef Iberica. Under the arrange-ment, Olazabel would make and sell Magic Chef ranges, sup-plying the factory, labor, and sales connections, while Magic Chef provided the designs, engineering, and some capital.

To make a go of the venture, Magic Chef would need to

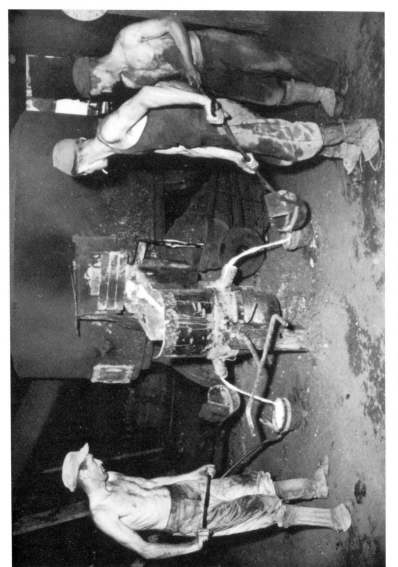

Molders at Dixie Foundry "pouring off" molten iron from the cupola.

The Eli Rymer family outside their cabin in Greasey Creek, Tennessee: left to right, Malinda, Bradford, Boyd, and Eli.

Workmen of the Quick Meal Stove Company, predecessor of the American Stove Company.

S. Bradford Rymer, age fifty-five.

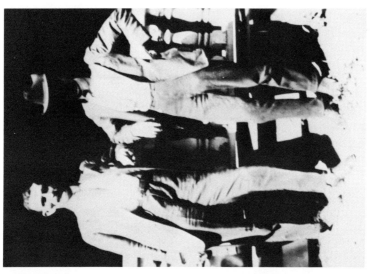

William Rohlman, Dixie's first ironmaster, stands beside Brad Rymer, whose face is lost in shadow.

Jefferson Davis Hanks helped draw the foundry's first heat.

"Quick Meal"

Gasoline Stoves

AND

Blue Flame Oil Cook Stoves.

1898

TRADE MARK

QUICK MEAL

"QUICK MEAL" No. 985.

EVAPORATING STYLE.

This is a grand, solid Range, gotten up without regard to cost. It is the most complete Gasoline Range ever produced, large enough for any family, restaurant or hotel. The difference between it and the Range on the opposite page consists only in the addition of the Step. For further description, sizes and weight, see next page.

TELEGRAPH
CODE WORD,

No. 985. CARMINE, Closet and Step Range....................$33 00

(*Left*) A gasoline vapor stove offered by Quick Meal in 1898. (*Right*) Quick Meal's trademark, a newly hatched chick in hot pursuit of a butterfly.

Dixie Foundry Company

Dog Irons

	8 in.	10 in.	12 in.	14 in.	16 in.
Wt. per pair	15½	16½	18½	19½	21

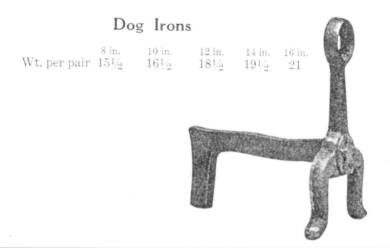

Sad Irons

Sizes 5 - 6 - 7 - 8 lbs.

Cleveland, Tennessee

Among Dixie's first products were dog irons and sad irons, illustrated in a page from an early catalogue.

Dixie Foundry Company

Bigwood Box Heaters

THIS is unquestionably one of the most sturdily constructed Box Wood Heaters on the market. It is designed to give maximum strength and lasting qualities. It is full size in every detail, as you will observe from the actual dimensions and weights shown. All sizes with swing top. Sides of No. 36 made in two pieces. All bolts are outside.

Dixie Foundry Company

C DIXIE OAK

IN designing "DIXIE OAK" Heaters we have aimed at simplicity, and at the same time building it to meet the requirements of those demanding maximum snap so far as appearance is concerned.

All parts used in construction of the Dixie Oak Heater shown above interchange with castings used in A and B styles illustrated on opposite page. This line of Oak Heaters give the buyer three styles to select from.

Dixie Foundry Company

"DIXIE KING"
Cannon Heater with Drum

"**D**IXIE KING" embraces the very last word in a heavy, large, efficient Cannon Heater. Full size according to number, large feed door with screw damper, swinging ash door with lever handle. Made with a heavy draw center and shaking grate, which can be quickly removed without dismounting the stove.

This stove is an ideal heater for use in stores, offices, schools, warehouses and other places where stoves are subject to hard usage.

(*Left*) In 1919 Dixie produced its first appliance, a wood-burning stove. (*Right*) During the early twenties the company came out with cannon heaters, or pot-bellied stoves, including the Dixie Oak and the Dixie King.

A molder at Dixie pours iron into his sand-filled flask.

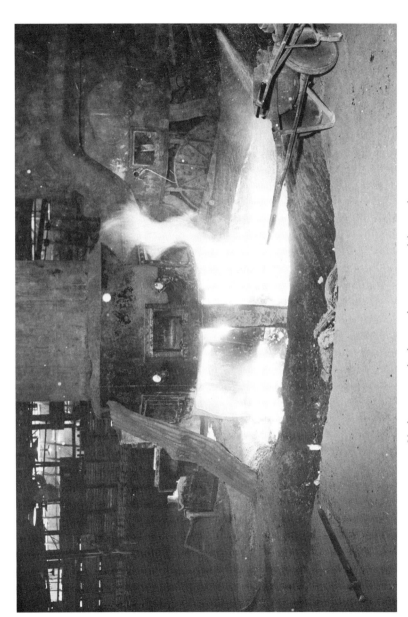

Used pig iron and coking coal empties out of the cupola.

A "shake out" man, Henry (Blue) Wells, removes finished castings from flasks in preparation for grinding and polishing.

In 1921 the company produced its first cooking range, a wood- or coal-burner called the Dixie *Larine*.

General White, Dixie's resident "genius with wood."

Brad Rymer, flanked by his sons, in 1938: left to right, Marvin, LeRoy, Brad, Robert, and S. B. (Skeet), Jr.

Clara LaDosky Gee, wife of Brad Rymer.

In 1925 these workers at Dixie polished nickel-plated parts on the machines at right. The men (left to right) are: Raleigh Stepp, Harve Nipper, Dewitt Slaughter, Roy Bass, W. R. Hayes, Lake Ledford, and Letch Jones.

MAGIC CHEF

Lends Character
to Any Kitchen

UNLESS the gas range has
a RED WHEEL it is not a
LORAIN

"MAGIC CHEF," the new vogue in gas ranges, lends character to any kitchen. And the character of the kitchen, more than any other room of the home, reflects the character and taste of the owner.

The sparkling, colorful beauty of "Magic Chef" transforms any kitchen, large or small, old-fashioned or modern, plain or colorful, into a charming, inviting room.

Moreover, in addition to its incomparable loveliness, "Magic Chef" embodies many unusual time- and labor-saving features, including the famous Lorain (Red Wheel) Oven Heat Regulator.

"Magic Chef," the first cooking appliance to be designed along ultra-modern lines, has quickly won the unqualified approval of gas-engineering and home economics experts, as well as the unstinted praise of authorities on design and interior decoration.

You'll find "Magic Chef" on display on the sales floors of dealers and gas companies throughout the United States. You are cordially invited to inspect it at your earliest convenience.

Showing "Jonquil" Model of Magic Chef in Modern American Kitchen

AMERICAN STOVE COMPANY ·· DEPT. B, 43 CHOUTEAU AVENUE, ST. LOUIS, MO.
Largest Makers of Gas Ranges in the World

Patents Pending

If gas service is not available in your community, let us tell you how to obtain tank-gas-service for use in a Red Wheel Gas Range

1. "JONQUIL" Model shown above in Old Ivory with Peacock Green trim. Also, "PATRICIAN" Model in Italian Grand Antique Marble finish with Old Ivory trim. Handles of Onyx Green Bakelite.

2. The "Magic Chef" Oven is equipped with the famous Lorain (Red Wheel) Oven Heat Regulator.

3. Cooking-top cover spring-balanced, easy to operate. Unsightly utensils quickly covered.

4. "Magic Chef" Oven is insulated. Keeps kitchen cooler when baking.

5. Pipes, gas valves and all bolts concealed. All valves convertible into "safety" valves.

6. Unique Broiling-feature includes an extension carriage that brings broiling pan into full view for the easy turning of meat. Reversible broiling pan requires no rack.

7. Top-burners of new, vertical-injection type have removable, non-corrosive heads. Each burner can be used as a simmering or a giant burner.

8. Roomy service-drawer on rollers.

CASH-PRICE
$195.00

($210 West of the Rockies)
Arrangements can be made
to pay out of income.

Send your name and address for
free copy of booklet showing modern kitchens.

Magic Chef

PRODUCT OF
AMERICAN STOVE COMPANY

During the late twenties, American Stove came out with a line of stylish gas ranges called Magic Chef. Advertisements such as this one proclaimed Magic Chef the "new vogue in cooking."

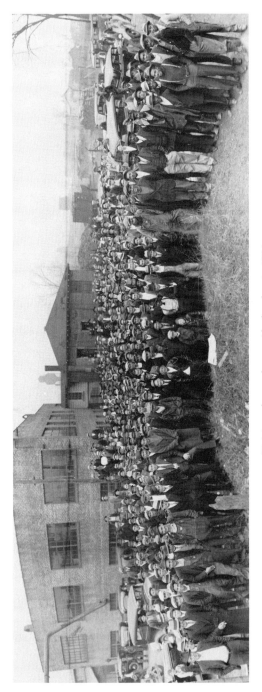

Dixie's workers gather outside the plant in 1934.

Marvin Rymer, vice-president in charge of sales, 1933–1962.

LeRoy Rymer, chairman of the board, 1959–1973.

S. B. (Skeet) Rymer, Jr., chief executive officer, 1950–1987.

Robert E. Rymer, secretary and treasurer, 1940–1973.

ON STRIKE

LEGAL STRIKE
CALLED. BY.
INTER-NATIONA L.
MOLDERS UNION.
STAY. A WAY
LOW. WAGE,S.
BAD. CONDITIONS
UN-FAIR. TO. UNION,
LABOR.

During 1937 and 1938, strikes were called at Dixie by the Congress of Industrial Organizations and by the American Federation of Labor. An unidentified picket stands outside the plant in 1937.

Employees gathered at a Christmas dinner in 1953.

Gas ranges move along the assembly line at Dixie, circa 1950s.

Workers in Dixie's gas-range department gather for a photograph in 1953. The man with the plaid shirt and glasses, kneeling in the center foreground, is Fred Nipper, long-time head of the department.

(*Top*) The Admiral Corporation, formed in 1934 as a manufacturer of radios, began to produce refrigerators in 1945 at a plant in Galesburg, Illinois. (*Bottom*) Admiral's Galesburg plant converted to the production of parachute flares, shell casings, and other war goods during World War II.

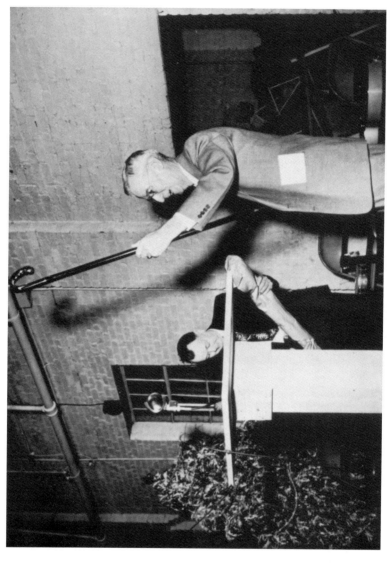

Brad Rymer, age 74, holds aloft a new cane given him by Dixie's employees

THE BRAND NEW *Magic Chef* GAS RANGE
all the modern conveniences you ever dreamed of

(*Top*) Skeet Rymer signs the agreement to purchase Magic Chef: left to right, Cecil M. Dunn, LeRoy Rymer, Skeet Rymer, Robert Rymer, and H. L. Dethero, who took charge of sales at the Magic Chef plant in Franklin, Tennessee. (*Bottom*) Magic Chef's trademark, a Disney-like creature dressed in formal attire and wearing a chef's hat, appears in an ad of 1948.

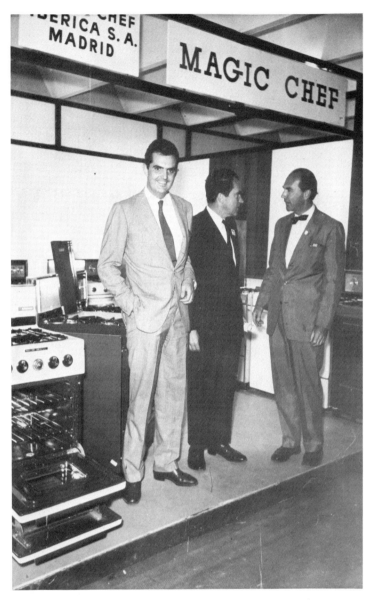

Barcelona, Spain, 1963: A.D. (Dick) Adair, Jr. (at right), head of the company's international operations, chats with Richard M. Nixon, while Jaime Olazabel, vice-president of Magic Chef Iberica, poses for the camera.

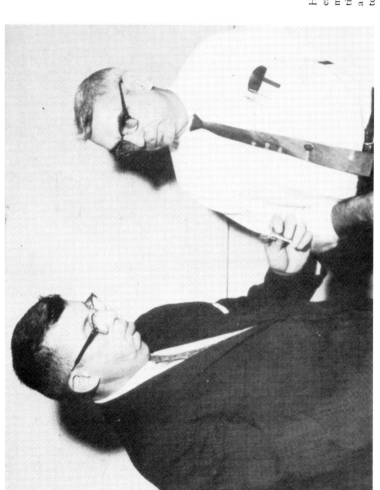

Harold Moss (at left), chief engineer, and Fred Heselmeyer, engineer for international operations, look over a new gas-range ignition system.

On February 25, 1970, Magic Chef's common stock was listed for trading on the New York Stock Exchange. Standing on the trading floor are (left to right) NYSE President Robert W. Haack, Skeet Rymer, Robert Rymer, and Herbert M. Aibel, who handled trading for the company.

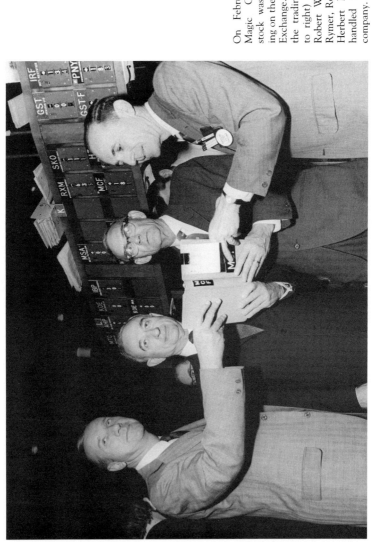

(*Top*) In 1979 Magic Chef purchased the Admiral Division of Rockwell International, which included this 1.3-million-square-foot plant in Galesburg, Illinois. (*Bottom*) Coinciding with the purchase of Admiral was the purchase of the Norge Division of Fedders, whose principal plant is this one-million-square foot facility in Herrin, Illinois. With the purchases of Admiral and Norge, Magic Chef became the nation's fourth largest appliance maker and a *Fortune* 500 company.

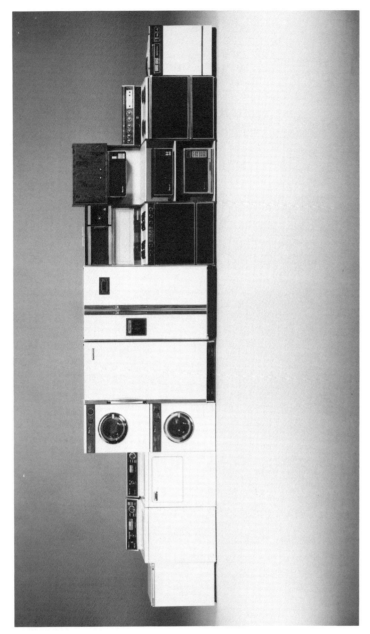

A selection of the full line of appliances made and sold by Magic Chef in 1980.

Magic Chef's directors, assembled in 1984: (seated, left to right) Carl Navarre, Howard L. Clark, Jr., S. B. Rymer, Jr., Roy T. Musselwhite; (standing, left to right) J. Hoyle Rymer, Willard F. Rockwell, Jr., John M. Templeton, Robert E. Rymer, and John R. Greene, Jr.

J. Hoyle Rymer, president of the Magic Chef Company, 1986–

transplant the latest American technology into a plant whose equipment and techniques were of pre-World War II vintage. That task, which demanded equal measures of technical competence and diplomacy, fell to an old hand from American Stove, Fred Heselmeyer, who joined Adair in Madrid as project engineer. Like all top-flight engineers, Heselmeyer was passionate about exactitude, but in his case the passion was tempered by an easy-going disposition, which undoubtedly helped him maintain his sanity. If an Iberica worker spied a wire whose function was a mystery to him, Heselmeyer recalled, he was as apt as not to cut the wire without a second thought. Quality control was to be a neverending battle. But with Adair and Heselmeyer riding herd, Magic Chef Iberica commenced production in March 1963, turning out the first ranges that its parent company had taken a direct hand in manufacturing abroad.

The investments in Pan Pacific and Magic Chef Iberica had been made during a period when declining sales and profits could easily have prompted management to retrench rather than expand. Hit hard by the side effects of reorganization, profits had fallen by eighty percent in 1961, and sales that year and the next contracted by twenty-five percent from the level of 1960. But these were birth pains, signs of new life. In 1963 the company rebounded, earning $3.49 million, before taxes, on sales of $29.8 million. Business reached a new plateau of $40 million in 1964, and, of equal note, 92 percent of that business derived from retailers and building contractors: the company had left private labeling. For two years—eight fiscal quarters—Rymer had accepted eroded earnings in return for solid gains in performance.

From two companies Rymer had forged one, which now handled more than twice the sales volume of its two predecessors combined. It was an impressive achievement, but Rymer spent little time admiring what had already been done. His mental docket was crowded with unfinished business, and one item in particular had absorbed him since 1960 or earlier: taking the company public. So long as one hundred percent of Magic Chef's stock stayed within the family's control, Rymer told the board in 1960, the company could not hope to attract the managerial talent and capital required to sustain its dynamic rate of growth. As Rymer commented later: "There are different reasons for going public. A lot of times it's not in your best interest, but other times it is. You find basically that family businesses have a tough time growing, maturing, and surviving from generation to generation."

As matters stood in 1960, however, Magic Chef was in no position to tap outside sources of capital and talent. Going public was not an option then, according to a study of the company conducted by Courts & Company, whose report concluded that "there is little interest in a closely held family controlled business which pays a modest cash dividend."

During the intervening years, management had taken steps to change that. In anticipation of going public, the Rymer sisters had left the board, to be replaced by Mills Lane; dividends had gone up; a profit-sharing program and a stock-option plan had been put into force; and one executive office had been filled by a man from outside the family, Roy Musselwhite.

Its image revamped, Magic Chef offered 272,000 shares of its stock to the public on May 5, 1964. If the directors worried about the reception, they need not have. Confirming Lane's prediction, the issue was oversubscribed, the bulk of it going to institutional investors such as Chemical Bank, Bank of America, Chase Manhattan Bank, and, of course, C&S National.

In taking the company public, as in adopting a nationally known brandname, the directors were redefining their business. With this and subsequent stock offerings, they were closing, if not locking, the door against temptations to keep Magic Chef a small, family business.

Less than a month after the stock issue, Skeet Rymer laid before the board two plans for expansion. The first one, as Rymer described it, involved only "normal capital expenditures without any acquisitions." This would yield a "growth rate of ten percent per year for a total sales volume of $50 million to $55 million by fiscal year 1969." But Rymer had no use for that plan, except as a means to sell the board up to his second, more ambitious plan. "It is entirely possible," he said, "to achieve sales of $90 million to $100 million or greater through a program of acquisition and merger." He proposed to buy the company's way into a new but compatible line of products. Among the possibilities were range hoods, garbage disposers, dishwashers, compact refrigerators, outdoor grills, and central heating and air conditioning. The board bought the deluxe plan, and Rymer went shopping for a company with annual sales of at least $10 million and operations that were profitable or that could be made so in one year.

Although Rymer hoped to locate such a company within two years, the search took a good deal longer than that. While it went on, Magic Chef advanced on several fronts. In January of 1965, Dick Adair set up another foreign subsidiary, Magic Chef Italiana, which produced and sold ranges and small refrigerators in a joint venture with a family of Italian manufacturers named Boggio-Sella. The year 1967 brought a major expansion to the Pan Pacific division when, in August, construction began in City of Industry, California, on a new 75,000-square-foot plant which would double available space. And a month later, Pan Pacific produced the company's first microwave ovens, commercial models designed for use in restaurants. Developed by Raytheon shortly after World War II, microwave ovens generate high-frequency radio waves that penetrate food and cause water molecules inside to vibrate quickly, thereby creating enough friction to cook most dishes in roughly a quarter of the time required by conventional methods. Lingering doubts about the ovens' safety had inhibited sales, but Magic Chef, together with most of the appliance industry, was betting that sales would take off within the decade.

Rymer's search for an acquisition took a definite direction in the summer of 1968, thanks to a useful piece of intelligence supplied by Mills Lane. The president of Republic Corporation, Jerry Block, had stopped by C&S National, Lane told Rymer, to shop for financing to ease Republic through some cash flow problems. During the visit, Lane learned that Republic owned an appliance manufacturer, Gaffers & Sattler (G&S). If Republic needed to raise cash, Lane suggested to Rymer, then perhaps Block would be willing to sell G&S. As Rymer discovered, Block was willing and eager to do just that, and in October Magic Chef concluded an agreement for the purchase. The largest manufacturer of ranges on the West Coast, G&S offered Magic Chef the chance not only to carve out strong sales territories west of the Rockies but also to diversify into a new line of products, central heating and air conditioning equipment.

But by no means did G&S present a ready-made opportunity. It had not shown a profit in five straight years. Moreover,

Magic Chef strained its finances to pay for G&S, whose purchase price of $17.4 million exceeded Magic Chef's net worth. That and the urgent need to revive G&S created what Rymer described as "shockwaves throughout our organization." In 1969, Rymer told an officers' meeting that "Gaffers & Sattler will stand on its own two feet. It will be operated as a separate corporation, paying its own way and paying off the loans made to buy it."

To that end, management streamlined the company, spinning off its water heater division and centralizing production. In June 1969, an up and coming executive at Magic Chef, William N. Austin, took charge at G&S. By 1971 the company would show a profit for the first time in eight years. Taking note of that showing, financial analysts at Smith, Barney & Company termed it "an impressive turnaround."

In another action that undoubtedly caused analysts to sit up and take notice, Magic Chef in 1969 added to its board a man whose name was spoken with awe in financial circles: John Marks Templeton. Alongside Templeton's story, the rags-to-riches tales of Horatio Alger seem like pretty dull stuff. As a young man without influential backers, Templeton had left his home in Winchester, Tennessee, worked his way through Yale during the Depression, studied law at Oxford on a Rhodes scholarship, and in 1939 borrowed ten thousand dollars with which to launch himself into the investment business.

On Wall Street, Templeton showed a wizardry for picking winners among the world's least known and most undervalued stocks. While the investment pack chased the latest glamor issues, Templeton ventured into the contrarian jungle, discovering and buying neglected bargains that would yield handsome returns. As a result, his mutual funds did things that mutual funds are not necessarily supposed to do, such as consistently outperform the Dow Jones Average. The Templeton Growth Fund, for instance, produced an annual rate of return of 14.7 percent over thirty years, from 1954 to 1984—"one of the best, if not the best record of any growth fund," judged the *Wall Street Journal.* Templeton was beating the market, a feat that according to efficient market theory is impossible. To explain what was going on, the business press began to speak of Templeton's "Midas touch."

In 1969 Templeton sold the bulk of his growth funds in order to devote more time to an interest that had captured his imagination: furthering spiritual progress in the world. Moving his home and headquarters to a porticoed mansion on Lyford Cay in the Bahamas, Templeton divided his time between business affairs and the establishment of an annual prize like none other. Called the Templeton Prize for Progress in Religion, it was richer by several thousand dollars than the next largest prize, the Nobel. The first award, presented at London's Guild Hall in 1973 by Prince Phillip, went to Mother Teresa of Calcutta, six years before she received the Nobel Peace Prize. To select Mother Teresa and later recipients, Templeton assembled a panel of judges including such luminaries as the Dalai Lama, President Gerald Ford, Yehudi Menuhin, Norman Vincent Peale, Duchess Josephine of Luxembourg, Mrs. Anwar el Sadat, and Edmund Leopold de Rothschild.

The man with the Midas touch who showered the saintly with gold, John Templeton was not a name likely to appear among the directors of an appliance manufacturer in Cleveland, Tennessee. And, as a rule, he declined invitations to serve on corporate boards. But since the early fifties, when he and Skeet Rymer had met in the Young Presidents Organization, they had formed a close bond. Each admired the other's achievements, and they shared an abiding faith in the Protestant virtues of hard work and self-reliance, free enterprise, and the Divine will. For Templeton, Magic Chef exemplified American business at its best, and he readily accepted Rymer's proposal to join the company. As a board member, Templeton did more than merely lend the considerable prestige of his name. A working director, he served on both the executive committee and the audit committee, giving Rymer the benefit of tips from one of the greatest financial minds of the age.

Owing to the purchase and revival of G&S, Magic Chef closed out the decade of the sixties with sales approaching $100 million. From the vantage of 1970, Dixie Foundry seemed a distant relative to the company now taking shape. That company had not only made a name for itself in the appliance industry but was also well on its way to becoming one of the nation's leading businesses. Confirmation of that came on February 25, 1970, when Magic Chef's stock was listed for trading on the New York Stock Exchange. A few days before Magic Chef went on the big board, Skeet Rymer spoke to a gathering of financial analysts in New York. He entitled his speech "From Cast Iron Skillets to Wall Street," emphasizing that the company had come to prominence out of nowhere. But lest any of his audience leave with the impression that Magic Chef was claiming to have arrived, Rymer ended his speech with a disclaimer: "Our attitude is one of progressive dissatisfaction. We have no intention of slackening our momentum."

8.

Testing the Limits

TO HEAR MANY of Cleveland's stove-company executives tell it, Skeet Rymer was going to break Magic Chef by pushing it too hard, too fast. Sales during the sixties had nearly quadrupled from the level of 1959, and some observers wondered whether such rapid growth would destabilize the company. But moderating the pace was the last thing on Rymer's mind. In September of 1970, even as Bill Austin struggled to keep Gaffers & Sattler in the black, Rymer hit the acquisition trail again. This time, his goal was to buy a company with $50 million in annual sales, or roughly the same volume of business that Magic Chef had been doing two years ago, before the purchase of G&S.

The following spring, Rymer spotted a likely candidate, the Johnson Corporation, headquartered in Bellevue, Ohio. Founded in 1958 and headed since 1967 by William Olsen and Gerard Miller, the Johnson Corporation made and sold central heating and air conditioning equipment, about $45 million worth a year. Because its primary markets were in the Midwest and Northeast, Johnson would complement, not compete with, G&S's strength on the West Coast. If combined with G&S, it would allow Magic Chef to distribute heat-and-air equipment on both sides of the Rockies—to take another product line nationwide.

It was, however, an opportunity that carried risk, for

Johnson was, according to President Olsen, "disturbed." Said Olsen, "we'd been doing a great deal of military business. It was well over half our sales one year and the next year we were out of it." Johnson had lost money in 1970, but Rymer thought highly of Olsen and Miller, whom he described as "one of the strongest management teams in the heating and air conditioning industry . . . [with a] philosophy much the same as ours."

As Olsen and Miller viewed the proposed merger, Magic Chef's financial resources and its operation at G&S offered them a much wider scope for expansion. The combination made sense to them, and on August 23, 1971, Johnson's stockholders sold the company for 525,000 shares of Magic Chef, worth $17.3 million at the time.

Rymer left Olsen and Miller in charge at Johnson, and though he conferred with them often and monitored performance closely, he did not superimpose his own managers on their organization. This genuinely decentralized approach worked: Johnson came back stronger than ever in 1972, when its pre-tax margins increased to 7.4 percent, from 2.5 percent the previous year. With net income of $1.9 million, the subsidiary contributed about fifteen percent of its parent's total earnings in 1972. Pleased with that showing, Rymer placed the management of G&S's heat-and-air business under the Johnson Corporation.

Since 1968 Magic Chef had bought $100 million in sales, but its staff in Cleveland had grown hardly at all. Corporate advertising and public relations were still handled by two men working out of a small office. In-house attorneys were unknown, all legal matters being handled by Francis Shackleford and, later, by his partner at the Atlanta firm of Alston & Bird, B. Harvey Hill, Jr. No phalanx of executive vice-presidents separated Rymer from frequent contact with the heads of various divisions; in fact, he would soon have fourteen divisional heads reporting directly to him. Some business observers doubted whether this lean, radically decentralized organization could administer the staggering increases in business. Those doubts were put in the form of a question to Rymer when he appeared before the New York Society of Security Analysts on November 11, 1971.

"Mr. Rymer," asked one analyst, "the sales which your corporate headquarters has administered over the last three years is about tripled. What changes, if any, have you made in your office to deal with this burgeoning sales growth?"

"I believe," Rymer answered, "in a philosophy of decentralized management . . . in assigning responsibility to the chief executive officer [of a subsidiary or division], along with giving him full authority to conduct his program. I don't mean that they have full authority to do anything they want to do. [There are] guidelines and we're in close communication with each other and we have a very good understanding. But I don't believe in setting up handicaps and roadblocks that hinder a person from making decisions and moving forward."

Evidently expecting to hear something more, the analyst followed up with another question: "And that's worked OK so far, and you have no reason to think that—any changes'll have to be made?"

"That's about it," Rymer agreed.

Rymer granted the divisional heads considerable latitude, even at times, as he himself admitted, letting them "push" him along against his better judgment. Yet no one seems to have mistaken this tolerance for weakness, at least not for long. When his patience wore thin, Rymer knew how to say no without leaving a trace of ambiguity in the mind of his listener. Said one divisional head, "Skeet ran a tight ship in a loose, relaxed way."

A strong believer in individual initiative, Rymer was dead set against creating an administrative apparatus that would hold everyone accountable to an elaborate system of checks and balances. Although he introduced the company to a formal method of planning and of measuring individual performance, known as Management by Objectives (MBO), he made it plain that there would be no gold stars for those managers who dreamed up complex and super-subtle refinements of MBO. "I don't think," he told a meeting of general managers in 1971, "that we should, as time goes by and we become more skillful, make MBO so sophisticated that those involved, including maybe us, get lost in the details. We must keep our eye on the objective."

And for any general managers who might think that their power within the company derived from the number of perquisites they commanded or the number of people who reported to them, Rymer had this to say: "We are not in the business of building a hierarchy, but of manufacturing and selling products. We must keep our fingers on the pulse by not isolating ourselves from employees and customers. Luxury fringes such as elaborate offices are monuments to someone's ego, and have a strong tendency to isolate people."

Rymer practiced what he preached. His own staff consisted of one secretary, Betty Harvey, and he worked out of an office starkly devoid of the usual trappings of executive power. Missing from it were such standard appurtenances as the massive desk and high-backed, throne-like swivel chair; or the ornate bookcase decorated with a few antique objects and richly bound volumes; or the team of receptionist and executive secretary who usher the visitor from one waiting area to another and finally into the inner sanctum. In fact, a visitor could walk straight into Rymer's office, and one who did, a financial analyst down from New York for his first visit with Rymer, was so mystified by what he found there that he initially mistook Rymer for a cost accountant. The analyst saw a bare linoleum floor of brown-and-white tiles, fluorescent lighting that would not have been out of place in a workshop, a gray steel desk with matching armchairs and a credenza along which ran a row of vinyl ring binders fat with pages. Though austere, it was a clean, well-lighted place, eminently functional and equally suited to putting a foreman at his ease or causing divisional managers to think twice before decorating their offices in the imperial motif.

About the only design schemes that the managers and Rymer had time for in 1971, however, were those affecting the company's manufacturing capacity. A two-year boom in appliance sales had left Magic Chef's plants straining to keep up with demand. To boost capacity, Rymer and his managers were drawing up plans for a costly program of expansion and technological uplift at the plants in Cleveland, Tennessee; Bellevue and Columbus, Ohio; Los Angeles and City of Industry, California; Turin, Italy; and a new factory in Anniston, Alabama which had taken over production of microwave ovens from G&S in January. Initial financing came from a stock offering of March 1972, that raised $20.5 million, and by 1977, when most of the program had been carried out, Magic Chef would have 3.4 million square feet of plants and 4,500 employees in four states.

In Cleveland, the team of Harold Moss, Charles Chavis, and Jerry Ward oversaw the construction of what came to be known as the West Plant, which contained its own fabrication, assembly, and enamelling units and amounted to a separate plant, hooked into the older one by an underground tunnel and miles of overhead conveyors. Completed in 1973, it would increase capacity by 25 percent, to 3000 ranges a day.

As the building campaign got under way in 1972, several events occurred that brought into sharp relief the company's origin, development, and destination. Chief among them was the closing of the corporate birthplace. It was there on a July afternoon during World War I that Brad Rymer, Dave Hanks, and a crew of molders had drawn the first heat from a second-hand cupola. For most of the company's history, the foundry had been its vital center—the one part that could stand for the whole; many old-timers still referred to Magic Chef as "the foundry," much as the entire executive branch of the government is encapsulated in the term "the White House."

But over the years, cast iron components had slowly given way to less expensive ones fabricated of steel or aluminum. During the same time, iron molders had seen their calling slip from a mainstay of American industry to a vanishing craft. By 1971, only one piece of molded iron went into Magic Chef's ranges (the burner grate), and engineers were already assembling a new machine that stamped grates out of steel. Once the company had employed some three hundred molders, but their ranks had thinned to twenty-two men in 1972.

Those twenty-two molders and many of their retired predecessors, men who had been known to one and all by such nicknames as "Knockout," "Peanut," "Taillight," "Bad Eye," and "Ground Hog," whose rite of initiation for the novice molder was to grease his ladle handle on the sly and watch the results—all these men gathered on the afternoon of February 29, 1972, for the foundry's last heat.

Those who poured the iron that afternoon included Clyde

Beaty, Joe Browder, Earl (Fletcher) Colloms, Grover Cooley, L. A. Evans, Clarence Hampton, Roy Huskey, Avery Johnson, Sam Leek, Bill McClure, John Olsson, Harold Ogle, Charles (Smokey) Owenby, and Cecil Tallent. Also in attendance were company officials, business and civic leaders, and a host of reporters.

While the television cameras rolled, the crowd watched as L. A. Evans and LeRoy Rymer tapped out the boiler of molten iron and as the molders poured the white hot liquid into their waiting flasks. After the last ladleful, the cupola's drop bottom was released, and the remaining coke and pig iron cascaded out in an eruption of sparks, smoke, and steam. Thus ended the tradition out of which the company had been born.

With the foundry's demise, a new piece of machinery became the main attraction on tours of the plant. Where once visitors had paused in wonderment to watch the cupola disgorge molten iron, they now directed their keenest attention to a block-long row of interlinked presses, known as the transfer, or "pacer," line. Installed at a cost of $1.4 million in 1972, the transfer line was composed of five 250-ton presses, synchronized so as to accomplish in one continuous operation the dozens of steps ordinarily spread out over numerous subassembly stations. A ten-ton sheet of coiled steel, fed in at one end, would pass automatically down the line and through a complicated series of stamping, bending and shearing dies, to emerge at the other end as a finished part.

Coinciding with the advent of the transfer line and the foundry's end were two retirements which further served to remind old hands at Magic Chef that the company was losing links to its past. On September 16, 1971, LeRoy Rymer, eldest son of the company's founder and, in point of service, its senior most executive, retired as chairman of the board. LeRoy had been present almost from the creation, seeing the company grow, he told the press, "from a small maker of cast iron pots and pans with a one-mule wagon to haul our merchandise to the depot, to what it is today." LeRoy's retirement was followed in 1973 by that of his fifty-two-year-old brother, Robert, secretary and treasurer and a driving force behind the highly successful mobile home-RV division.

Of the four brothers who had grown up with the company and assumed its executive offices, only Skeet remained. The brothers, like all brothers, had not always seen eye to eye. But now that LeRoy, Marvin, and Robert were gone from management, Skeet occasionally felt their absence. There was no one left in the company with whom he could talk as freely and openly as he had with his father and brothers. His sense of solitude could only have been deepened by the death in November 1973 of Francis Shackelford, the company's first outside director, its general counsel, and Rymer's close advisor for twenty years.

Early one Sunday morning toward the end of 1973, Skeet telephoned one of his nephews, Robert's twenty-nine-year-old son Hoyle, and invited him to join Magic Chef as his assistant. Skeet had kept track of his nephew's development, and he liked what he saw. A graduate of the McCallie School in Chattanooga and of Davidson College, Hoyle had picked up an MBA from Emory University and served a two-year hitch in the Army, including tours of duty in Viet Nam and at the Pentagon. Then, moved by the spirit of social activism prevalent in the late sixties, he signed on as a staff member in the office of the Secretary of the Department of Health, Education and Welfare. But there he soon grew disenchanted with what he termed "much talk and no action," and in 1971 struck out on his own, joining with two friends to operate an oil and gas exploration firm, National Resource Management Corporation, based in West Virginia.

In his nephew's varied background, Skeet saw at least two qualities he admired: an entreprenurial bent and the self-reliance to move outside the circle of family connections.

At first, Hoyle greeted his uncle's invitation with something less than enthusiasm. Business was good in the oil patch and, besides, Skeet stopped short of saying exactly what job he was offering at Magic Chef. Even so, upon reflection Hoyle began to feel, as he put it, "unable to pass up an opportunity to join the company that had been so much a part of the family." In December he agreed to give Magic Chef a try, and with that embarked on a career that in the fullness of time would have a considerable effect on the company's development.

When Hoyle Rymer arrived at Magic Chef in January of 1974, the company had entered a period of lean years. The first in a succession of misfortunes had come on March 16, 1973, when a flash flood swamped the plant, submerging the new transfer line and causing $350,000 in damage as well as loss of precious production. Two months later, management was forced to eat another $682,000, which had been invested in plans to make refrigerators at a new plant in Anniston, Alabama, using technology to be borrowed from Magic Chef Italiana. But Italiana's engineering standards, Skeet Rymer belatedly concluded, would not yield a refrigerator likely to pass inspection by Underwriters Laboratories, let alone the buying public. Apart from the monetary loss, this aborted project dashed any hope of broadening the company's line of kitchen appliances, a move which was becoming imperative now that many buyers insisted on outfitting kitchens from wall to wall with a single line of appliances.

October brought a crushing blow. When war erupted in the Middle East, the Organization of Petroleum Exporting Countries (OPEC), embargoed oil going to the United States and other allies of Israel. In no time the American economy, already weakened by inflation, faltered badly as doubts about the sufficiency of oil supplies undermined public confidence. Homebuilding, on which Magic Chef depended for much of its sales, contracted sharply, and in November orders had dwindled to the point where management laid off 300 of the company's 2300 employees at the Cleveland plant.

The OPEC embargo also gave rise to the perception that the nation, deprived of major sources of oil, would soon exhaust its supplies of natural gas. In consequence, the demand for gas ranges plummeted as consumers opted to buy electrics. Magic Chef, more than most appliance makers, suffered from the trend toward electrics. The company was particularly vulnerable because seventy percent of the ranges it sold were gas fuelled, whereas the appliance industry as a whole went into 1973 selling a healthier mix of sixty percent electric and only forty percent gas.

Figuratively, the guns along the Suez had fired a salvo into Magic Chef: during the last quarter of 1973 its sales fell off $5 million and its profits were off $1.9 million from the same quarter in 1972.

There was scant cause for optimism, either. In December 1973, analysts at Paine Webber predicted that in the year ahead the "prospects for appliance sales [would be] grim."

At Magic Chef, 1974 was a year of curtailed production, layoffs, and three-day work weeks. The economic indicators that mattered most told a dismal tale. Sales of mobile homes skidded thirty percent. Consumers, tightening their purse strings, spent less and less on replacing old appliances with new ones. Housing starts in December dipped to 880,000 units—the lowest figure recorded since the government had begun to keep track of construction in 1946. For the year's final quarter, Magic Chef posted an operating loss of $835,233.

Despite the heavy going, Skeet Rymer followed through on the plans laid in better times to expand manufacturing capacity. As was typical of Rymer, once he committed himself to a program of investment, he saw it through even at the immediate cost of depressed earnings. Earlier, he had accepted two years of spotty performance in order to push through the consolidation of Dixie and Magic Chef. And, unlike some executives known for taking a meat axe to new acquisitions that operated at a loss, Rymer showed a willingness to invest in ailing subsidiaries rather than merely cut costs to the bone. Taking note of Rymer's tendency to stick it out through the worst, his son-in-law, the historian Frederick Turner, half jokingly called him a "desperate optimist." Rymer explained his attitude another way: "When times are bad, you can see the weak spots better, you can build cheaper, and you can be ready for the upturn, which will surely come."

Events sorely tested that philosophy. When Moss and plant manager Jerry Ward revved up the West Plant, sales volume no longer warranted the added manufacturing horsepower. Having overbuilt, the company was stuck with the expense of maintaining excess capacity.

At the microwave oven division in Anniston, problems of quality control and productivity bedeviled management, preventing the company from seizing the one advantage to come its way from the OPEC oil embargo. While the embargo had dampened enthusiasm for gas ranges, it had also spawned demand for energy-efficient appliances, especially microwave ovens. Nationwide, microwave ovens were one year away from generating more sales dollars than gas and electric ranges combined. Given this trend, Rymer considered it possible that microwave ovens would replace gas ranges, even as gas ranges had spelled the end of coal-and-wood burners. At the least, something new had come out of the appliance industry and taken the nation by storm, but Magic Chef was watching it all from the sidelines.

Rymer assigned to his nephew Hoyle the job of straightening out the kinks in Anniston. Upon Hoyle's recommendation, the division disposed of its commercial line of models, designed for restaurants and food-vending businesses. These commercial markets, where sales volume was low, did not fit into the company's system of distribution, and to develop them would entail creating a new sales force at an expense hardly justified by potential profits. Instead, Hoyle would concentrate on mass producing residential models of top quality, which could be merchandized through the company's existing channels to appliance dealers, builders, and mobile home manufacturers. In order to achieve manufacturing economies at Anniston, the company invested heavily in new equipment and engineering with which to increase production and improve quality. Among Hoyle's first steps was to recruit the assistance of Fred Gant, a soft-spoken but intensely determined engineer whom Hoyle knew from high school days. Together, they raised production from 100 units to more than 2500 units per day in a few short years.

Stagnant economic conditions, coupled with sizable expenditures at the plants in Anniston, Cleveland and elsewhere, siphoned off earnings during the second and third quarters of 1975. At year's end, Magic Chef wound up in the red, registering a loss of $1.875 million—its first since the depression year of 1932.

The figures improved somewhat in 1976, but it was not until the following year that Magic Chef broke out of the cycle of setbacks that had begun with the flash flood in 1973. But when the upturn came, it was apparent that the company had sustained no lasting damage during the more than three years of assorted reversals. In 1977 operations not only regained their former vigor but two lackluster divisions emerged from the hard times as potent moneymakers. That was the conclusion reached by Blyth Eastman Dillon in a report of 1978, which noted: "Magic Chef ended fiscal 1977 with sales and earnings fully recovered from the effects of the recent recession. The company's pre-tax margins by line of business have also retraced spreads lost since 1972, and two formerly marginal products, microwave ovens and vending equipment, have been developed into profitable growth areas."

The investment made at Anniston had paid off, for the microwave division had become the fastest growing segment of Magic Chef's business. Its sales during fiscal 1977 were up by eighty percent, as compared to a gain of only sixty percent by the industry as a whole. To give sales a further push, management decided to underwrite a lavish advertising campaign aimed at a national audience. At the time, endorsements by baseball great Joe DiMaggio were brewing up heady sales for Mr. Coffee machines. It was this that led Skeet Rymer to telephone one of his neighbors at Lost Tree Village, Florida—professional golfer Jack Nicklaus. Would Nicklaus and his wife, Barbara, star in Magic Chef's advertising spots? Nicklaus agreed, signing a promotional contract that allowed some of his celebrity to rub off on Magic Chef's products.

Over the next years, the business relationship between Rymer and Nicklaus ripened into friendship, which would continue even after Nicklaus ceased to represent the company in 1987.

Not far behind Anniston was a division whose performance had once been so consistently poor that efforts were made to dispose of it: Dixie-Narco. Through the 1960s Dixie-Narco's annual sales had remained flat, at $2 to $3 million. That had changed in 1971, when Magic Chef bought Carl Navarre's fifteen-percent interest in the vending machine maker. Until then, the Navarre Corporation had exercised control over sales of Dixie-Narco's products, limiting their distribution to Coca-Cola bottlers. But with Navarre bowing out, sales were consolidated with manufacturing under the direction of Roy Steeley, long-time president of Dixie-Narco. It was a reorganization that Navarre supported wholeheartedly. Steeley, at last given the chance to call all the shots, put his sure grasp of the industry to good use. He fused sales and manufacturing into a formidable combination, and he went after the business of soft drink bottlers formerly off limits: Dr. Pepper, Pepsi Cola, Royal Crown, and Seven-Up. As a result, Dixie-Narco outstripped many of its larger competitors, such as Westinghouse, Vendo, and Cavalier, and in 1976 the subsidiary earned $1.2 million on sales of $14.1 million. Steeley had turned a piece of cut glass into a tiny but exquisite jewel, the smallest but most profitable part of Magic Chef.

Rymer fared less well with his experiments in international manufacturing. Despite the best efforts of Dick Adair, backed up by engineer Fred Heselmeyer, the Spanish and Italian operations never quite lived up to expectations. Returning from a visit to Magic Chef Iberica in 1967, Rymer delivered to the board a report tinged with frustration and resignation: "Progress in Spain is painfully slow. This, I am convinced now, is the nature of the people and the country. They are just now getting into production (I hope) the new ranges which were just going into production on my last visit. I suppose the most important thing decided was setting the objective of next June 30 to have a successfully operating company—or else."

After enduring a few more of Iberica's false starts, Rymer decided that he might as well look for the tooth fairy as for progress out of Spain. Accordingly, he took Magic Chef out of the Spanish operation, focusing then on the Italian subsidiary. There, too, promises and projections consistently outran results. Something always knocked earnings for a loop; either the Italian government was suing to collect enormous back-tax claims, which Rymer considered totally unjustified, or else inflation was driving interest charges up to 24 percent. As a last ditch effort, Magic Chef underwrote a $4 million loan to its subsidiary in 1975. Sales ballooned, but Italiana sustained a pre-tax loss of $1.9 million.

Deciding that good money was being thrown after bad, Rymer retained Citicorp's international banking department to find a buyer for Magic Chef Italiana. After contacting twenty-three companies in Europe, the bankers at Citicorp reported no interest in Italiana. One Italian company said that because the subsidiary "had not been profitable even in years when it should have been possible to make profits," it would consider the purchase only on condition that Magic Chef agree to provide a support fund for Italiana. An Italian industrialist allowed that he "would not give one lire" for Italiana under any conditions. The best deal the bankers could scare up was with the subsidiary's Italian principal, Edoardo Boggio-Sella, who agreed to buy Magic Chef's interest for a "negative consideration," meaning that Magic Chef would pay him to take the company. Given the lack of alternatives, the bankers at Citicorp advised Rymer "to proceed with all speed to the formalization of the proposed transaction with Edoardo Boggio-Sella." Rymer did just that in December of 1977, thereby closing out the company's last venture in international manufacturing.

For Rymer, the failure abroad was a pinprick compared to the serious shortcoming that had caused him mounting pain since the mid-1960s. Magic Chef was a single-line company in a business increasingly dominated by full-line companies, or those that made a complete selection of kitchen appliances. As Rymer explained the problem: "Dealers and housewives want all their appliances to have the same brand name. You'd walk down a store aisle and see refrigerators, ranges, washers, and dryers from GE lined up together. Then there'd be Magic Chef in a corner with a few ranges. Why fool with us for just one product?"

The one-product companies not only found it difficult to compete with the likes of GE and Whirlpool, they were also failing or being gobbled up like peanuts. Rymer had watched as Raytheon picked up Amana Refrigeration in 1965 and Caloric two years later. Then he had seen White Consolidated snap up six appliance companies between 1967 and 1977: Hupp, Studebaker's Franklin division, American Motors' Kelvinator, Athens Stove Works, Westinghouse's appliance division, and finally Ford's Philco line. The day of the single-line company was drawing to an end.

Looking for a way out of the one-product trap, Rymer in 1977 made a bid for the Norge division of Fedders, which manufactured clothes washers and dryers. But he backed off when it occurred to him that refrigerators, not laundry equipment, had to be the cornerstone on which to build a multiline company. Unhappily for Magic Chef, it lacked the wad of capital, which Rymer estimated to be $150 million, necessary to build a refrigerator plant from scratch. And none was up for sale. Increasingly, the company's sales force encountered dealers who refused to order Magic Chef ranges when they could obtain the full array of appliances from other companies. As matters stood, in order to field the semblance of a full line, Magic Chef resorted to the practice of buying refrigerators and other appliances from competitors, then branding and selling these goods at a slight markup. At best, it was a precarious and marginally profitable way of doing business. The company's prospects looked increasingly doubtful in an industry where, as Rymer put it, "the future belonged to the full-line manufacturers."

Rymer always liked to say that "luck is where preparation and experience meet opportunity," and in July of 1978 he received a telephone call during which precisely that happened. On the line was his old friend from the YPO, Al Rockwell, who proceeded to offer Rymer what a financial analyst at Merrill Lynch later called "perhaps the last opportunity . . . for Magic Chef . . . to get ready-built factories to broaden their product line." Rockwell proposed to give Rymer first crack at buying an ailing subsidiary of Rockwell International: Admiral.

Once, Admiral had dwarfed both Rockwell's company and Rymer's. But that was a long time ago.

Although a child of the Depression, Admiral had grown out of the more expansive, boom-or-bust tradition of the Roaring Twenties. The company was conceived in Chicago by the son of a Sicilian bootmaker, Ross David Siragusa.

His first business venture, a company that made battery chargers, had gone belly up in 1934, leaving Siragusa deep in debt. Scraping together $3,400 that year, he teamed up with his cousin, Vincent Barreca, to make five-tube radios and sell them at depression prices: $9.95 apiece.

Siragusa and Barreca tasted success early. After two years of business their company—which had started out in a borrowed garage—was doing $2 million in sales. The partners had hit on a winning formula. By underpricing most of the competition, they had managed to latch on to a small chunk of the fast-growing radio business, where industry sales had increased from virtually nothing in 1920, when the nation's first radio station went on the air, to $842.5 million in 1929. Their ambition whetted by success, Siragusa and Barreca expanded Admiral rapidly, producing an array of radios, hi-fis, and phonographs. In 1941, sales hit $9.3 million. That, however, was only the beginning.

In 1944, after only a decade in business, Siragusa, who by then dominated Admiral, decided that the time had come to branch out aggressively. He rightly expected the demand for appliances to erupt at the end of World War II. In order to capitalize on this bonanza, he readied Admiral to deliver not only radios and phonographs—called "brown goods" in the industry—but also "white goods": ranges, refrigerators, and other kitchen appliances.

Toward the end of 1944, Siragusa acquired the refrigerator division of Stewart-Warner Corporation. The next year he contracted through Kalamazoo Stove for the manufacture of a line of Admiral ranges, on top of which he paid two million dollars for the inventory and machinery of a company that wanted out of the electric-range business: Pressed Steel Car, of Pittsburgh. In 1948 Siragusa added yet another product, television sets, and during 1950 he bought a plant in which to make refrigerators, the Midwest Manufacturing Company, located in Galesburg, Illinois. Within six years' time, Siragusa had brought out a line of ranges, a line of televisions, and a line of refrigerators.

By the standards of the appliance industry, new products were streaming out of Admiral like confetti at a tickertape parade. The company's profits, which had stood at $3.6 million in 1948, skyrocketed to $18 million in 1950. It was a rich haul, but one that Siragusa would never see again. As consumer demand tapered off, so did Admiral's profits. Worse still, there were signs that the company had grown large without having grown up.

It leaned heavily on the charismatic leader and on gutsy instinct to compensate for its immaturity as an organization. In 1951 the advertising department produced an unsigned article in which the question of maturity was raised and then dismissed with two-fisted bravado. The article noted: "Ross David Siragusa . . . is the man who runs the show. He has broad shoulders and an athletic frame. He is dressed smooth as silk. He is doing a tough job in a tough business. . . . Ross Siragusa readily accepts the friendly warnings of his competitors that he is fast becoming a big boy, and that big boys must take care. His executive setup is too thin. This is no good for a company pushing to sell above the $100-million mark, and Ross Siragusa proposes to do something about it. In the meantime he will do the best he can with what he has."

But it was not quite that simple. Years later, Siragusa himself looked back and reflected: "It was between 1948 and 1951 that we forgot about the necessary research and engineering that we needed. We overlooked it because we were too excited about the future and didn't prepare properly."

Admiral's management never succeeded in undoing the damage done. In 1957, when profits dropped below $1 million, the company ceased to pay dividends. During the mid-1960s, Siragusa attempted to merge Admiral into the Chrysler Corporation, but nothing came of it. Occasionally the company had a good year, but overall its sales and earnings eroded steadily. It lost $3.8 million in 1967, and in 1970 it posted a devastating loss of $16.1 million.

As Admiral floundered, the Rockwell International Corporation went shopping for companies that would allow it to decrease its dependence on the aerospace and defense business. The plan, masterminded by Al Rockwell, was to buy into the consumer goods business, staking out claims in both brown goods and white goods. Within a sixteen-month period, Rockwell made three major acquisitions, ending with the purchase of Admiral for $79 million in April of 1974. It was a transaction that, according to the pronouncements of all parties involved as well as some accounts in the business press, would give Admiral what it needed most: the financial backing and engineering might of a giant such as Rockwell.

But the marriage proved shaky from the start. Even as it was consummated, the Japanese were moving full tilt into the brown goods market. The foreign invaders "hung Rockwell International out to dry," observed *Forbes.* Admiral, during its first nine months under Rockwell's umbrella, lost $16.2 million.

There was also the problem of compatibility. Appliance makers operate on slim profit margins in an industry where cost overruns cannot easily be passed on to customers. Of necessity, most appliance makers were sticklers about efficiency, long before productivity became a buzzword and a fashionable subject of study in the larger business world. But a different situation prevailed in Rockwell's primary business.

In aerospace and defense contracting, it was not unusual for a project to go over budget, and the government often picked up the tab for cost overruns.

The record also suggested that Rockwell was fishing in troubled waters. Other industrial Goliaths had already taken a drubbing in the appliance business. American Motors cast off Kelvinator in 1967. Ford would dump Philco in 1977, and General Motors would discard Frigidaire in 1979.

As Admiral continued to sputter despite liberal aid from Rockwell, several business observers speculated that Rockwell was not coming to grips with the harsh realities of the appliance business. The same point was made more bluntly by an assembly line worker at Admiral's Galesburg plant, who later remarked, "it was spooky the way Rockwell spent money here."

In 1977, moving to cut losses, Rockwell jettisoned Admiral's least profitable unit, the television division, which had piled up a deficit of $73.7 million since 1974. Although performance improved, Admiral continued to run at a loss in 1978. By then, the board of directors of Rockwell International was pressing Al Rockwell to dispose of Admiral and other money-losing consumer goods subsidiaries.

Skeet Rymer was eager to disburden his friend of Admiral. Negotiations began in July, dragged into August and September, at which time Rymer checked himself into the Miami Heart Institute for coronary bypass surgery. While still confined to a hospital bed, he used the telephone to pick up the thread of negotiations. At the same time, he was once again angling to purchase Norge, a feasible acquisition provided that Magic Chef could add refrigerators to its product line. Upon release from the hospital, Rymer repaired to his winter home in Lost Tree Village, Florida, where he met with agents from both Admiral and Norge. Nailing down both companies, he later said, was his "project while recuperating in Florida."

By January, Rymer had worked out an agreement in principle to acquire Admiral, and, during the next month he hammered out terms for buying Norge from Fedders. What Magic Chef proposed to pay for the two companies—just over $70 million—was, according to Rymer, a sum considerably less than the replacement value of their assets. But as more than one director pointed out to Rymer, that outlay would break Magic Chef if the company failed to bring off a quick turnaround at Admiral. In taking on Admiral and Norge, Rymer would, one director reminded him, be risking all that he and his family had built up over the years.

Rymer assayed the risks somewhat differently. "The risk of not doing it," he later said, "would have been greater than the risk of doing it." Assuming the worst, that Admiral could not be put back on its feet—a possibility that he considered unlikely—then the losses would steadily eat up earnings and credit, eventually forcing the sale of Magic Chef. But even in this extremity, he believed that an unprofitable full-line company would be more valuable than a profitable single-line company—that Magic Chef would be "stronger with Admiral than without it." And so Rymer proceeded to put Magic Chef on the line, with the unanimous backing of his board.

In May of 1979 the stockholders acted, approving the purchase of Admiral for $58.6 million, as well as the purchase of Norge for $13.25 million. When the deals were closed, Magic Chef became the nation's fourth largest appliance manufacturer, behind General Electric, Whirlpool, and White Consolidated.

Whether Magic Chef could digest its new acquisitions and then use them to compete head-on with far larger companies were questions much discussed in the nation's business press. The company was bucking stiff odds. Analysts were predicting an economic slowdown that could clobber the appliance business, along with Magic Chef's chances of reviving Admiral and Norge. And even if the company succeeded there, it might still lack the size and margins necessary to compete against the kingpins, General Electric and Whirlpool, each of which had over $2 billion in sales, compared to Magic Chef's $400 million.

Generally, financial analysts hedged their bets on the outcome, ending up with such predictions as: "More than one company has been very successful in one area of business and struggled like hell when it ventured out of its niche." While these observers judged the situation strictly in terms of accepted business theory, others looked closely at the personalities involved. Said James Magrid, vice-president of Shearson, Loeb: "Skeet Rymer is a good, tough, hard-nosed businessman. There are few executives in the appliance industry as smart as he is. Other guys in his position would have been broke by now."

Still another vote of confidence came from a reporter sent by *Forbes* to interview Rymer in June of 1979. Weighing the pros and cons of Magic Chef's situation, the reporter wrote: "Skeet Rymer shows a flinty east Tennessee tenacity that smoother corporate executives lack. 'We're appliance people,' he says. 'It's our only business, and we're totally committed to it. I think we're big enough and efficient enough now to compete with anybody.'" The reporter concluded his article with this observation: "How much credence would a security analyst put in that [statement], compared to the hard facts of Magic Chef's objective situation? He would probably prefer the hard facts—and thereby disregard the crucial element that no less an authority than J. P. Morgan found all-important in making a loan. 'Character,' he said, 'comes before anything else.'"

9.

Design for Tomorrow

SOME TWENTY YEARS had passed since the day Skeet Rymer told the directors of Dixie Foundry: "We can go forward or we can go backward. But we cannot stand still." Time had done nothing to weaken that resolve to strive without pause. Indeed, it had become almost an article of faith that the company was only as good as its next achievement. With the back-to-back acquisitions of Admiral and Norge, Rymer, at age 64, had put that vision to the ultimate test. Standing still was no longer an option for Magic Chef.

Out on the dangerous edge, Rymer worked to minimize and control the risks. His instinct was to merge Admiral into Magic Chef, thereby lessening the overhead and internal friction generated by two organizations operating in parallel. But his earlier experience in combining Dixie and Magic Chef caused him to go slow. The dislocations arising out of that earlier merger had knocked sales off by forty percent. A loss of similar magnitude now would be fatal. Rather than chance it, Rymer decided to live with the less than desirable arrangement until such time as the two companies were strong enough to undergo merger.

The immediate problem was to rescue the new subsidiaries without drawing so close to them as to be caught in a deadly embrace. Results had to be obtained at arm's length. To that end Magic Chef applied the techniques of decentralized management that it had been perfecting for decades. Rockwell International, having grown anxious for results, had shuffled managers in and out of Admiral so fast, Rymer noted, that "none of them ever had time to dig the company out." Rymer stopped the revolving door. He installed one of Rockwell's men as general manager, John R. Greene, Jr., who would soon be given charge of Norge as well.

Greene, urged on by Rymer, thinned out the bureaucratic undergrowth that distracted attention from manufacturing and marketing fundamentals. He reduced staff by seventy-five percent, and he disposed of Rockwell's labyrinthine system of controls which, he concluded, "did not permit us to control our overhead." To track every nut, bolt, and man-hour at Admiral made about as much sense as inventorying the cargo on a sinking ship.

As the subsidiary slimmed down, Magic Chef funneled millions of dollars into a program to build up Admiral's manufacturing muscle. Among the larger outlays, $10 million underwrote the construction of a 400,000-square-foot warehouse and distribution center at Galesburg, and $8 million went into an automated paint system there. These investments came as most appliance makers were hunkering down, bracing for the effects of soaring interest rates, which were dampening consumer spending and housing starts. In May of 1980, as the prime rate approached 21.5 percent and appliance shipments fell off by one-third from the previous May, General Electric idled 11,000 workers, and Whirlpool trimmed its workforce by 4,000. Under the circumstances, *Business Week* termed Magic Chef's heavy investments a "recession defying gamble." Typically, though, Rymer was taking the long view, spending money to reduce manufacturing costs and thus be ready for the upturn, which he never doubted "would surely come."

In taking on Admiral and Norge, Rymer stretched not only Magic Chef's financial capacity but also its management resources. At the Cleveland headquarters a staff of fourteen now administered eight thousand employees spread over ten plants in six states. Rymer himself logged thousands of air miles monthly, shuttling from one plant or meeting to the next. One week, for instance, he flew into New York on a Saturday, stayed over through Monday, then touched down in Galesburg on Tuesday, departing there in time to spend Wednesday in Anniston. Getting by on four hours sleep a night was not unusual for Rymer. He had managed to drive himself relentlessly since 1950, thanks to his iron constitution and his understanding wife, Anne. The soul of patience, Anne had compensated for her husband's absences from the family circle, while using her social grace to help him cultivate friendships of benefit to the company.

Although he still possessed the stamina that had earned him his nickname as well as the envy of men half his age, Rymer did not kid himself. In 1979 he began to delegate the burdens more freely than he had before. He named Hoyle Rymer president of the Magic Chef division, which included the plants in Cleveland and Anniston. In 1980 he caused the board to elect William Austin president and chief operating officer of the corporation. But this executive realignment was not entirely successful, for Austin resigned within the year.

Given the company's tradition of one-man leadership at the top, Rymer found it impractical to select a second-in-command. To do so would be the same as designating his heir apparent; so he left the post vacant. But he relied increasingly on three officers: chief financial officer Al Rohrbaugh, who had been of inestimable value in upgrading fiscal policies but who was nearing retirement; as well as two younger men—Hoyle Rymer, 36, and John Greene, 46. Moreover, Skeet had taken care to assemble a board that was much more than a ceremonial body. Several of the outside directors were recognized as creative geniuses in the world of business and high finance. As a group, they constituted a powerful brain trust. Besides John Templeton, the outside directors included Carl Navarre, a pioneer in the use of leveraged buyouts, who had put together one of the nation's larger Coca-Cola bottling enterprises. Navarre's financial savvy, and Templeton's, had been enormously valuable as Rymer acquired companies with net worths greater than Magic Chef's.

It was also through Navarre that Rymer had met another director, Howard Clark, Jr., managing director of Blythe Eastman Paine Webber, Inc. Clark, who would soon join top management at American Express—which his father had headed for some twenty years—brought to Magic Chef a sure grasp of investment banking. Rounding out the list of outside directors was Al Rockwell, who had built a $5-billion company and, along the way, handed Magic Chef the opportunity to grow into a full-line appliance maker.

Over the years Rymer's business relations with each of these men had ripened into friendship, further strengthening their ties to the company. Characteristic of the directors' loyalty was a declaration that John Templeton once made privately to Rymer. In the unlikely event of a serious disagreement, Templeton told Rymer, he would quietly resign rather than speak or vote against his friend.

For Rymer, the board room was a calm center during the otherwise stormy years of 1979 and 1980. One reason for worry was the threat that Admiral and Magic Chef might cross swords. Some skirmishing was inevitable, but if war erupted it would destroy both companies. Keeping the peace was critical, and, more often than not, breaches were handled not with naked force but with diplomacy. At one point, discord between the two sales forces reached such a state that some managers at Cleveland insisted that marketing efforts be consolidated under them forthwith. The logic was right but the timing was wrong, Rymer told his managers. Still, the issue remained alive and became a focus of contention between the sales managers at Magic Chef and Admiral.

A rift in marketing was not far from the last thing Rymer needed in 1980. To avoid it, he retained a consulting firm for the announced purpose of conducting a thorough and impartial study. Out of it would come recommendations that would settle the matter once and for all. After a few months of intensive study, the consultants handed in their report. They concluded that the existing sales structure was the best possible. The sales managers, acknowledging that outside experts perhaps had seen the situation more clearly than they had, dropped the issue, though every now and then they puzzled over the outcome. Rymer never gave it another thought. He had guided the consultants to their conclusion from the beginning.

By the end of 1980, Rymer's strategy—peacemaking ploys and all—started to pay off. In spite of the deepening recession, Admiral turned a small profit—no mean achievement, considering that the company had lost $180 million during five economically more favorable years under Rockwell International. At Norge, performance approached the break-even point. There, however, years of inadequate investment in technology had exacted a high toll, which could only be reversed by sustained spending over the long haul.

When the results for 1981 were in, it was evident that management had indeed succeeded in recreating Magic Chef as a full-line company. At $674.2 million, sales had nearly doubled since the acquisitions, and profits hit a high of $16.2 million. The gains, far from being soft growth, proved remarkably hardy. As the nation's economy continued to unravel, Magic Chef's sales held together, decreasing by only two percent in 1982.

What many observers had viewed as a gamble now appeared in a new light. "Rymer seems to have guessed right," concluded *Business Week* in June of 1983. "In a downturn for the industry as a whole last year, Magic Chef's sales held stable, and analysts expect record sales of more than $700 million for fiscal 1983. . . . Such a performance has helped triple Magic Chef's stock price in a year."

Besides that, Magic Chef held the distinction of being one of the only single-line companies to have emerged from the appliance industry's shakeout as a full-line manufacturer, an honor that it shared with Raytheon and White Consolidated. As a further mark of success, Magic Chef's name appeared on the list of the nation's five hundred largest industrial corporations—in the band of titans known as the Fortune 500. It stood in 415th place and would rise some one hundred places in the next three years. In recognition of the company's singular progress, *Dealerscope Merchandising,* citing the fact that Rymer had "built a small appliance firm into a megacompany," selected Rymer as one of the nation's "12 Marketing Legends," along with RCA's David Sarnoff, Panasonic's Raymond Gates, and Sony's Akio Morita.

One might reasonably suppose that Rymer had long since reached the point where he could rest easy in the knowledge that Magic Chef had come into its own. Asked in 1986 when he had felt that sense of well-being, Rymer replied: "I worry every day about survival. I've always been scared that the company wouldn't be able to compete in the marketplace, that some unforseen development would suddenly put us in jeopardy. All along, the company has had to play catch up with larger competitors. I always felt that it would fall behind if we didn't stay on top of it. You could say that a sense of anxiety has kept me running all my life."

According to one school of thought within Magic Chef, it was management's single-minded concentration on Admiral and Norge that gave labor unrest at Cleveland the chance to flare into a long and bitter strike early in 1983. There had been signs of growing trouble between management and organized labor, represented by the company's old nemesis, the International Molders Union. In three elections held between 1964 and 1970, workers at the Cleveland plant had overwhelmingly rejected the IMU's bid to organize them. But after the election of September 1970, which the IMU lost by a vote of 738 to 384, the contest became closer. In March of 1973 the IMU narrowly lost, by a vote of 716 to 633. Six years later, the union won by a slender margin, was certified as a bargaining agent, and in December of 1979 negotiated a three-year contract. Later, union officials told the *Wall Street Journal* they figured that they had won the contract partly because management's concern over Admiral and Norge made it a bad time for the company to risk a strike.

When the contract came up for renewal, union agents pressed for more liberal terms, arguing that management was paying higher wages at the Admiral plant in Galesburg than in Cleveland. Management countered by pointing out that wages and working conditions at Cleveland were as good as could be found in the area, and in most cases better. The union demanded a 37.4-percent increase in wages; the company offered 11.2 percent. Each side held fast to its position, and when the contract- expired on January 23, 1983, the IMU called a strike. Out of a workforce of 1,000 laborers, 575 IMU members walked off the job. The ensuing events eerily recalled the strike that Brad and LeRoy Rymer had faced in 1937.

In the eye of the storm this time was Hoyle Rymer, who, with Skeet's decisive backing, promptly hired new workers to replace the strikers. Hardly had the plant gone back into production than the dispute turned bloody, capturing national headlines. On February 2, a Chattanooga television personality, Judy Corn, was assaulted by a woman while seeking to interview an IMU official at the union hall. On February 23, Cleveland police lobbed tear gas canisters into a crowd of strikers who, as the official report put it, had "become unruly." Three days later, five thousand backers of the IMU paraded through Cleveland, down streets emptied of traffic, past stores closed for fear of violence. They converged on the houses of several company officials, including Hoyle Rymer's, where they chanted "Down with Rymer! We want a contract!"

Suits and countersuits were filed. In April the Atlanta office of the NLRB dismissed the charges of unfair labor practices lodged by the IMU against Magic Chef. Management, claiming to have documented 750 acts of union-inspired violence, sued the IMU for $20 million in damages. Meanwhile, the NLRB's Washington office was about to set aside the earlier ruling and order a rehearing of the IMU suit. Out of it would come a finding against Magic Chef, ordering management to re-hire more than 400 striking workers and give them back pay. But this verdict was not final. The court battles would continue for years, providing work for an army of law-yers and tying the parties up in a *Jarndyce* v. *Jarndyce* of liti-gation.

As the flurry of legal action began, terrorism of the sort ordinarily associated with Beirut or Belfast hit Cleveland. Nails were dumped on roads, shots were fired, hundreds of cars and trucks were damaged, and one employee's poodle was skinned alive. Each morning for weeks, some of Magic Chef's employees had regularly inspected their automobiles for the odd wire that spelled trouble. The practice became more widespread after May 13, when a charge of dynamite ripped apart a truck in the parking lot and damaged nine other vehicles nearby.

By this time, management and the IMU had met four times with a federal mediator, but talks had broken down. After the last session, on May 25, management unilaterally announced a wage increase equivalent to the final offer rejected by the union in January.

From this point, the IMU's strength began to evaporate. Its national boycott of Magic Chef's products had had no appreciable effect on sales, and regardless of who was answer-able for each and every act of violence, it had probably hurt the strikers' image most. In late August the head of the local molders' union, William Cubitt, confessed to the *Wall Street Journal:* "The union's gone. People for one hundred years will be scared to even mention the word union, much less organize people." On September 3, the union called off its strike.

Although the dispute would drag on through the courts for years, management had made its point: rather than buy temporary peace at the price of concessions deemed injurious in the long run, Magic Chef would take a strike and fight it to the bitter end. That refusal to back down ought not to have come as a surprise to anyone, though, for there was nothing in the company's history to suggest that management would have acted otherwise.

Neither the strike at Cleveland nor the challenge of digesting Admiral and Norge had stopped management from expanding into several new businesses. The first of these acquisitions was Revco, a South Carolina-based maker of freezers which Magic Chef picked up in March of 1981 for $15 million. Then, in September of 1983, the company paid $43 million for Toastmaster, whose books showed $100 million in solid sales. Headquartered in Columbia, Missouri, Toastmaster manufactured and sold small appliances such as clocks, fans, toasters, humidifiers, and heaters, which put Magic Chef into the housewares business.

Internally, too, the company was expanding. Nineteen eighty-four marked the beginning of a boom in sales of established products. When Roy Musselwhite retired in June of that year, Mike McDavitt was named senior vice-president of sales and marketing. McDavitt's strategy was to develop a more upscale market for the product line, by pinpointing exceptional dealers and offering them greater profit opportunities than could be had through mass-marketed lines. McDavitt's strategy paid off in short order: sales to independent appliance dealers more than doubled within two years.

Continuing to flesh out its product line, the company bought the Warwick Manufacturing Company during December 1984, in a $10 million deal that added compact refrigerators to Magic Chef's offerings. The next year $2 million went for the purchase of Ardac, Inc., a manufacturer of dollar-changing and validating machines, which dovetailed with Dixie-Narco's line of soft drink vending machines.

These new segments of business, on top of the business now coming out of Admiral and other subsidiaries, sent Magic Chef's sales past the $1-billion mark in 1984. The stellar performance did wonders for the company's earnings, which rose from thirty-one cents a share in 1980 to $5.55 in 1985. During the same period its stock price leaped by 900 percent, to $65 a share.

Paradoxically, such gains exposed the company to danger. Wall Street was rife with takeover artists who fed on the value that others had created, and some analysts insisted that with Magic Chef's stock selling at only eleven times earnings, the company was an undervalued and choice morsel. Charles Ryan of Merrill Lynch had begun to file reports touting Magic Chef as a likely target for corporate raiders. If the company were broken up and sold piecemeal, Ryan said, it would bring as much as $80 a share.

As it turned out, nobody attempted to seize and plunder Magic Chef. Nobody had the chance, owing largely to a course of action that Skeet Rymer took on December 16, 1985. It was then that he retained the investment house of Shearson Lehman Brothers to study the feasibility of reorganizing Magic Chef, either by taking it private, selling it outright, or merging it into another company. The threat of a hostile takeover, which bulked large in later accounts of the event, played a relatively small role in his decision. For at least three years, Rymer had been weighing what he called his greatest responsibility: "to position the company for the future." As far back as May 19, 1982, at a session of Magic Chef's executive committee, Rymer had outlined a plan which, in his handwritten notes, he titled "Sell Magic Chef at Proper Time." According to his notes, "the proper time would be when most of the consolidation plans are complete, economic conditions are again good, Magic Chef is making a good profit, and the price of the stock is satisfactory."

Then and later, Rymer, offered some compelling reasons for reorganizing the company. In his remarks to the executive committee in 1982 he noted that "of the five full-line major appliance manufacturers, Magic Chef has by far the least amount of resources available to it. Even Maytag has much more. If we are to succeed in a big way in the future, we must spend millions in product development and plant automation. Obviously, there must be additional capital, for all this cannot be done, I don't think, through profits and borrowings alone?"

Indeed, the competition from General Electric and Whirlpool had become ferocious compared to what it had been when Magic Chef ventured into the full-line market. From 1978 to 1980, General Electric had neglected its appliance business while debating whether to stay in it. But in 1981 the company had decided to spend $1 billion over five years to revitalize and automate its factories. Magic Chef, highly leveraged after years of acquisitions, could not begin to match this level of spending or that of Whirlpool. In 1985, GE also introduced a line of gas ranges, thus competing for the first time with Magic Chef's leading product.

Rymer had bucked stiffer odds before, but in 1985 he turned seventy. For almost fifty years he had devoted himself heart and soul to the company. Of those years he commented: "I was almost a prisoner here." As a captive, he had served eagerly, with great relish, and would undoubtedly have fought off any offer of parole. But the decades of zealous service had not left him with the sense that he was Mr. Magic Chef, perpetually indispensable and insistent on calling the shots until the last. The company, he believed, could continue without him. There were, nonetheless, Herculean labors awaiting anyone who stepped into his shoes, and Rymer did not wish to impose these on a single man. Not on his nephew Hoyle, whom insiders knew had the best chance at succession. And not on John Greene, whom Rymer had named president and chief operating officer in April of 1985. Rymer meant to spread the burdens more widely than in the past, and by so doing equip the company with the financial and managerial resources that it had never enjoyed but could no longer do without.

At first, Shearson Lehman turned up an investor who offered to acquire Magic Chef through a leveraged buyout. Such a deal ran counter to Rymer's intent, since the company would end up deeper in debt without anything to show for it. Even so, Rymer was tempted momentarily. "I could have run the company as long as I wanted, then quit," he explained. Shortly before the deal was to be concluded, Rymer realized that he was putting his own interests before Magic Chef's. As he later observed: "The company would have been weighted down with a tremendous load of debt. One little recession, and the company couldn't have met its debt service." With that concern uppermost, Rymer backed off from the deal.

Next, Shearson Lehman drew up a list of companies that represented attractive merger partners. At the top of the list Rymer placed a firm out of Newton, Iowa—the Maytag Company. Founded in 1893 as a maker of farm machinery, Maytag had since created a lucrative market for its top-of-the-line laundry equipment. But as Rymer knew, the company's chief executive, Daniel Krumm, was attempting without much success to move beyond the single product. In 1981 Krumm had acquired Cleveland's Hardwick Stove Company, then followed that up with the purchase of Jenn Air in 1982. The cornerstone of a full-line company, however, still eluded Maytag, for no refrigerator factory had come on the market since Magic Chef bought Admiral, and the chance of one popping up looked remote.

Krumm was later to comment: "The one thing we did not have was refrigeration manufacturing. Maytag has been very strong in the upper end of the market, but we have not participated in the middle of the market, where Magic Chef is very strong and where most of the sales occur."

On the other hand, Maytag possessed some assets that Magic Chef lacked. The Iowa company had a superabundant cash flow and an exceptionally low debt-to-equity ratio, which gave it the capital and credit to finance major expansions. It also had considerable depth in management, as well as what arguably was the most respected brand name in the appliance business.

On January 6, 1986, Rymer telephoned Krumm to suggest that they get together later in the week at a meeting they would both be attending in Florida. No topic of discussion was mentioned, but Krumm accepted the invitation with the certainty that more than a social visit was in store.

The two executives met on January 10, at the Breakers Hotel in Palm Beach. After they and their wives had dined together in the grand hotel, the two men retired to its elegant ballroom, where Rymer made his proposal. "Here we were," recalled Krumm, "in this huge room that holds hundreds. We went into a corner and talked in hushed tones."

From that point their discussions progressed rapidly, if in less regal and public surroundings. Within a month they met again and agreed on ground rules for the merger. After that, the matter was turned over to the bankers and lawyers, who acted with dispatch. On March 24, Magic Chef's board and Maytag's simultaneously approved the proposal. The last step was taken on May 30—Rymer's seventy-first birthday—when the stockholders of each company ratified the agreement. By its terms, Magic Chef's shareholders exchanged each of their 9.6 million shares for 1.671 shares of Maytag, a stock swap valued at $746.8 million.

It was a deal in which everybody stood to gain, Rymer predicted. "The two companies are stronger together," he said, "than either of them could have been apart." Wall Street overwhelmingly agreed, with analyst Charles Ryan speaking for the majority when he said: "I think both companies, once they began talking, realized that two and two would equal more than four, that it would be a very good combination."

For Magic Chef, it was pretty much business-as-usual in the months following the merger. The company operated as a semi-autonomous subsidiary of Maytag, and in an interview with the New York *Times*, Krumm said that he expected to maintain that status.

The most important change at Magic Chef took place so quietly that few noticed it. At the time of the merger, Skeet Rymer had announced his plan to retire on August 31, 1987, after a fifteen-month transitional period in which he would continue as Magic Chef's chief executive and also serve as chairman of Maytag's executive committee. Nothing much was made of Rymer's announcement, and in the following months the company treated his impending retirement as a minor news item, as just another event in the ordinary course of business. That was the way Rymer wanted it.

He steadfastly declined all proposals to make his departure

the occasion for ceremony. At his request, company officials cancelled a banquet at which he was to have been the guest of honor. Less formal tributes were likewise parried by the intended recipient. In the end, an out-of-town engagement prevented Rymer from visiting the company on the last day of his fifty-year career there. His decision to exit silently was understandable, for his feelings about the company ran too deep for easy expression at a time that seemed to call for his swan song.

His decision also carried on a tradition central to the company's success. The energy that might have gone into marking corporate milestones had always been applied to the business at hand. Instead of pausing to admire yesterday's triumphs, Rymer had encouraged an attitude of "progressive dissatisfaction" with what had already been done. It was the next achievement that mattered.

There were no speeches or accolades at Rymer's retirement, just as there had been none when Brad Rymer drew the first heat at Dixie Foundry. Both occasions exemplified the progressive discontent that has enabled the company to outdistance scores of larger rivals in one of America's most competitive industries. Looking back on the first heat, Skeet Rymer once described it in words that are equally appropriate to his own retirement: "It was a day like many others—marked not by ceremony—but by the dignity and satisfaction of hard work and by enthusiasm and initiative."

Chronology

1916   (August 24)   S. Bradford Rymer (b. 22 October 1879; d. 13 April 1959) and J. C. McKenzie incorporate the Dixie Foundry Company, with McKenzie as president, general manager, and secretary. Rymer serves as treasurer and puts up $5,000 to purchase a two-acre site for the foundry on the south side of Cleveland, Tennessee.

(November 1)   J. C. McKenzie, age 56, dies following a blood transfusion.

1917   (January 15)   Joining Rymer on Dixie's board are James P. O'Neal, John S. O'Neal, and Oscar Brown. Rymer soon arranges to rent the foundry, a sixty-by-sixty-square-foot tin-roofed building with a small cupola, to Jefferson Davis Hanks, president of the Hanks Stove & Range Company, of Rome, Georgia.

(July 16)   Hanks and Rymer draw the first heat. Among the products made are hollow ware, sugar kettles, wash pots, and grates.

(August 8)   The board issues fifty shares of Dixie to the Hanks Stove & Range Company.

1918   The directors are Brad Rymer (president), Hanks (vice-president), J. S. O'Neal (secretary), J. P. O'Neal, and Oscar Brown. Earnings for the year total $5,547.24.

1919   Production of heaters begins.

1920   The brothers O'Neal leave the board and are replaced by J. B. Brown and Mrs. S. B. Rymer.

1921   Dixie introduces a cooking range, the Larine, in coal and wood burning models. O. P. Brown and J. P. Brown resign and are replaced by A. H. Rogers and William Rohlman.

(September 15)   Grover Cleveland Brown joins the company as a director, sales manager, and treasurer.

1923   (January 12)   The directors decide to borrow money on the endorsements of Rymer and Brown in order to operate the foundry full-time. The minutes record that "the directors thought it would be wholly unwise to consider the paying of a dividend owing to the heavy indebtedness of the company."

1924   (January)   J. D. Hanks leaves the company.

(March 25)   On motion of Grover Brown, the board votes unanimously to surrender Dixie's corporate charter and to do business as a partnership between Rymer and Brown. No action is taken on the resolution.

1925   Sales total $452,571.

1926   Sixteen salesmen are paid commissions totalling $16,792.85.

1927   The directors surrender Dixie's corporate charter, and the company reorganizes as a partnership in which Rymer owns a 78.51 percent interest and Brown the remainder. LeRoy Rymer joins the company.

1928   Earnings total $87,692 on sales of $729,892.

1929   The company begins to manufacture gas ranges. Marvin Rymer goes to work in the crating department.

(February 6)   Fire destroys factory on east side of King Edward Avenue, causing $44,312.49 in direct damage.

1931   Earnings drop to $4,663.

1932   Operations sustain a loss of $6,230.15 on sales of $614,509.

1933   (November 29)   Brown sells his interest to Rymer and leaves the company. Marvin Rymer takes charge of sales.

(December 15)   Rymer re-incorporates the Dixie Foundry Company.

1934   First $1 million in sales brings a profit of $89,221. LeRoy Rymer is named general manager.

1937   (June 11)   The Congress of Industrial Organizations (CIO) calls a general strike that shuts down Cleveland's stove works. At Dixie, 650 workers walk out and picketing begins.

(July 9)   CIO pickets withdraw from Dixie.

(July 12)   A majority of workers having agreed to return to the job, Dixie reopens.

(July 25)   The International Molders Union, affiliate of the American Federation of Labor (AFL), declares a strike that shuts down Dixie. Management begins to hire enough new employees to put the plant back in operation. The IMU counters by filing with the National Labor Relations Board sixty-five complaints charging Dixie with unfair labor practices. S. Bradford (Skeet) Rymer, Jr. joins the company.

1938   (April 8)   Toward the end of the NLRB's hearing of the case of IMU vs. Dixie Foundry, Rymer signs a contract ending the dispute. Sales total $1.366 million, profits $61,620.

1939   Skeet Rymer plans and supervises the installation of Dixie's first motorized assembly line, as well as a reorganization of all departments except molding. Robert Rymer comes to work at the company.

1943   Sales reach $3.6 million, before-tax profits $1.036 million.

1944   Brad Rymer suffers a debilitating heart attack. The directors are Brad Rymer, his wife Clara, LeRoy Rymer, Marvin Rymer, Skeet Rymer, Robert Rymer, Zola Rymer Graf, Ruth Rymer Dethero, and Roberta Rymer Keyes.

1945   A two-year program of expansion begins at the plant.

1946   The company hires its first full-time engineer, Harold Moss. Steel shortages crop up nationwide, posing a threat to the company.

1947   An enamelling plant, headed by Ed Yarbrough, goes into operation.

1949   The manufacture of coal and wood burning stoves is discontinued; a re-designed and re-engineered line of gas ranges is introduced at the Chicago Furniture Market. Sales of $4.04 million bring a profit of $113,685.

1950   (January 1)   Skeet Rymer assumes the presidency as his father retires to the new position of chairman of the board.

1952   Management begins to phase out distributors and build a sales force that deals directly with retailers.

1953   (January 1)   By vote of the board, the company's name is changed to Dixie Products, Inc. The company begins to advertise its ranges in nationally circulated magazines, such as *Better Homes & Gardens* and *Sunset*.

1954   The company produces its first electric ranges.

1955   Francis Shackelford, a partner in the Atlanta law firm of Alston, Miller & Gaines, is elected a director. Sales stand at $11.2 million, profits total $641,285.

1956   The plant encompasses 500,000 square feet of space and sits on 24 acres. Some 60 tons of steel are processed each day, and the foundry pours an average of 25,000 pounds of iron daily.

1957   (May 28)   A foreign subsidiary is formed, Cocinas Dixie de Venezuela, headed by A. D. (Dick) Adair, Jr. and based in Caracas, Venezuela. The board also authorizes purchase of the Victor Products Plant, out of which is formed a subsidiary for manufacturing and selling soft-drink vending machines, Dixie-Narco, located in Ranson, West Virginia.

1958   (August 8)   Dixie buys Magic Chef for $1 million. The board decides to operate Magic Chef as a separate division of Dixie.

1959   (April 13)   Brad Rymer dies, at age 79.

1960   (December 6)   The company is re-named Magic Chef, Inc.

1961   (January 1)   Management begins to consolidate Dixie and Magic Chef.

1962   (March)   Roy T. Musselwhite succeeds Marvin Rymer as vice-president in charge of sales.

(August)   The board authorizes what turns out to be an unsuccessful attempt to acquire the commercial-range division of Waste King, Inc., which Waste King had earlier acquired from American Stove Company.

(October)   Magic Chef buys the Pan Pacific Manufacturing Company, a maker of ranges for recreational vehicles, located in Los Angeles, California.

The company organizes a manufacturing subsidiary in Madrid, Spain: Magic Chef Iberica, which is headed by Dick Adair and Jaime Olazabel.

1963   Construction begins on $2.5 million in additions to the Cleveland plant, which when completed in 1965, increases space by 100,000 square feet and expands manufacturing capacity to 1700 ranges daily. 76 percent of the ranges sold by the company are gas fueled, 24 percent are electric. Mills

B. Lane, Jr., president of Citizens & Southern National Bank, is elected to the board.

1964 (May 5)   The first public offering of Magic Chef's stock (272,000 shares at $16.50 apiece) is oversubscribed. Sales of $40.06 million yield a profit of $2.15 million.

1965 (January)   The company organizes Magic Chef Italiana, a manufacturing subsidiary in Turin, Italy, headed by Dick Adair and Edoardo Boggio-Sella.

Key managers at Cleveland include H. L. Dethero, vice-president of builder sales; Roy Musselwhite, vice-president in charge of sales; Harold Moss, chief engineer; Fred Heselmeyer, international engineer; R. E. Spruiell, director of manufacturing; Charles Chavis, superintendent of manufacturing; William N. Austin, director of industrial relations; W. C. Nevin, production manager; A. B. Miller, Jr., assistant secretary; James L. Taylor, Jr., purchasing agent; and J. L. Clemmer, assistant treasurer.

1967 (August)   Construction starts on a 75,000-square-foot plant for the Pan Pacific division in City of Industry, California.

(September)   Pan Pacific produces Magic Chef's first microwave oven, a commercial model designed for use in restaurants.

1968 (October)   Magic Chef pays the Republic Corporation $17.4 million for Gaffers & Sattler, an appliance manufacturer in Los Angeles.

1969 (June)   William Austin takes charge of Gaffers & Sattler.

Magic Chef's sales force of 145 men sell $90.4 million in merchandise; profits reach $3.1 million.

1970 (February 25)   The New York Stock Exchange lists Magic Chef for trading.

1971   (January)   The microwave oven division is transferred from California to a 40,000 square foot plant in Anniston, Alabama. Albert Rohrbaugh joins company as comptroller.

(August 23)   Magic Chef acquires the Johnson Corporation, an Ohio-based manufacturer of central heating and air conditioning equipment.

1972   The Cleveland plant comprises 725,000 square feet and employs 1,900 persons.

(February 29)   The foundry draws its last heat.

1973   (March 16)   A flash flood swamps the Cleveland plant, causing $350,000 in damage.

(May)   Management abandons plans to build refrigerators in Anniston using technology to be supplied by Magic Chef Italiana.

(November)   300 of the Cleveland plant's 2300 workers are laid off.

The company liquidates its interest in Magic Chef Iberica. Robert Rymer retires from management.

1974   Division heads reporting to Skeet Rymer are Roy Musselwhite, executive vice-president of Magic Chef; William N. Austin, president of Gaffers & Sattler; Roy S. Steeley, president of Dixie-Narco; A. D. Adair, Jr., chief of international operations; Edoardo Boggio-Sella, vice-president of Magic Chef Italiana; William Olsen, president of the Johnson Corporation; and J. Hoyle Rymer, general manager of the microwave oven division.

1975   The company registers a loss of $1.87 million.

(September)   The Frymaster Corporation purchases Magic Chef's line of commercial microwave ovens.

1976   (May)   William Austin succeeds William Olsen as general manager of the Johnson Corporation.

1977   Magic Chef operates 3.4 million square feet of plants and employs 4,500 persons in four states. Sales total $277.9 million, profits $13.7 million.

A national advertising campaign is launched, featuring Jack Nicklaus and his wife, Barbara.

(December)   The company liquidates its interest in Magic Chef Italiana.

1978   (July)   Skeet Rymer begins ten months of negotiation for the purchase of the Admiral division of Rockwell International and the Norge division of Fedders.

1979   (May)   Magic Chef buys Admiral for $58.6 million and Norge for $13.25 million, thereby becoming the nation's fourth largest appliance manufacturer.

1980   *Fortune* ranks Magic Chef the nation's 415th largest industrial concern. The board of directors is composed of William Austin, vice-president of Magic Chef; Howard L. Clark, Jr., managing director of Blythe Eastman Paine Webber, Inc.; John R. Greene, Jr., vice-president of Magic Chef; Roy T. Musselwhite, vice-president of Magic Chef; Carl A. Navarre, chairman of the Coca-Cola Bottling Company of Miami; Willard F. Rockwell, Jr., chairman of the executive committee of Rockwell International Corporation; J. Hoyle Rymer, vice-president of Magic Chef; Robert E. Rymer, retired officer of Magic Chef; S. B. Rymer, Jr., chairman and president of Magic Chef; and John M. Templeton, president of Templeton Growth Fund, Ltd.

The board elects William Austin president and chief operating officer, with Skeet Rymer continuing as chief executive officer.

1981   (March)   Magic Chef buys a manufacturer of freezers, the Revco division of Rheem (located in Williston, South Carolina), from City Investing Company for $15 million.

(August 27)   William Austin resigns as president and chief operating officer.

(September 1)   Magic Chef merges the East and West Coast heating and air conditioning operations into a new division headed by Gerald J. Kamman.

1982   The company employs 7,350 workers in seven states and has 6.26 million square feet of plants.

1983   (January 23)   When a three-year contract with the International Molders Union expires, a majority of Magic Chef's unionized workers go out on strike. Management immediately hires replacements. The IMU files complaints with the National Labor Relations Board charging the company with unfair labor practices.

(April)   Management files a $20-million suit against IMU Local 48.

(May 25)   Management announces wage hikes equal to the final offer rejected by the IMU.

(September 3)   The strike ends, though the dispute continues through the NLRB.

(September 15)   Management announces the purchase of Toastmaster, a maker of clocks, fans, toasters, humidifiers, and heaters, based in Columbia, Missouri.

1984   Sales exceed one billion dollars.

(June 30)   Roy Musselwhite retires as vice-president of sales and is succeeded by Mike McDavitt. A. H. Rohrbaugh, vice-president of finance and treasurer retires, to be succeeded by James A. Shoup.

(December 31)   For $10 million, Magic Chef acquires the Warwick Manufacturing Corporation, which makes compact refrigerators.

1985   (April)   John R. Greene, Jr. is elected president and chief operating officer.

(July 26)   For $2 million, the company purchases Ardac, Inc., which manufactures dollar-changing machines.

(December)   Skeet Rymer meets with investment bankers at Shearson Lehman to discuss re-structuring Magic Chef.

1986   (January)   Merger discussions begin between Skeet Rymer and Daniel Krumm, of the Maytag Corporation.

(March 24)   The boards of Maytag and of Magic Chef approve the proposed merger of the two companies. *Fortune* lists Magic Chef as the nation's 249th largest industrial concern.

(May 30)   Magic Chef merges into the Maytag Corporation.

1987   (August 31)   Skeet Rymer retires after fifty years with the company, thirty-seven of those years as its chief executive officer.

Selected Bibliography

Allen, Frederick Lewis. *Only Yesterday: An Informal History of the 1920s.* New York: Harper and Row, 1931.

————. *Since Yesterday: The 1930s in America.* New York: Harper and Row, 1939.

Barclay, R. E. *Ducktown: Back in Raht's Time.* Chapel Hill: University of North Carolina Press, 1946.

Bell, Daniel. *The Coming of Post-Industrial Society.* New York: Basic Books, 1973.

Blythe Eastman Dillon & Co. "Company Report: Magic Chef, Inc." 1978.

Caudill, Harry M. *Night Comes to the Cumberlands.* New York: Little, Brown and Company, 1962.

Chapman, H. H. *The Iron and Steel Industries in the South.* Birmingham: University of Alabama Press, 1953.

Clark, Victor S. *History of Manufactures in the United States.* 3 vols. New York: Peter Smith, 1949.

Corn, James F. "C. L. Hardwick: A Biographical Sketch." np, 1982.

Cowan, Ruth Schwartz. *More Work for Mother: The Ironies of Household Technology from the Open Hearth to the Microwave.* New York: Basic Books, 1983.

Dixie Foundry Company. Board Minutes, 1916–1960.

Eller, Ronald. *Miners, Millhands, and Mountaineers: Industrialization of the Appalachian South, 1880–1930.* Knoxville: University of Tennessee Press, 1982.

Encyclopaedia Britannica, 11th ed., s. v. "Founding."

Farnham, Charles F. "The Romance of American Stove Company Pioneers." Manuscript history. 1947.

Federal Writers' Project. *Tennessee: A Guide to the State.* New York: Viking, 1939.

Flexner, Stuart Berg. *Listening to America: An Illustrated History of Words and Phrases from Our Lively and Splendid Past.* New York: Simon & Schuster, 1982.

Forbes, R. J. *Man the Maker: A History of Technology and Engineering.* London: Abelard-Schuman Limited, 1958.

Graf, Zola Rymer. *A Family Chronicle of S. Bradford Rymer.* np, 1960.

Graham, Margaret Partlow. "Saga of the Gas Range." *What's New in Home Economics,* May 1945.

Hanks Stove & Range Company. Board Minutes, 1923–26.

Jacobs, Jay. *A History of Gastronomy.* New York: Newsweek Books, 1975.

Kephart, Horace. *Our Southern Highlanders.* New York: Macmillan Company, 1913.

Kondic, V. *Metallurgical Principles of Founding.* New York: American Elsevier Publishing Company, 1968.

Lifshey, Earl. *The Housewares Story: A History of the American Housewares Industry.* Chicago: National Housewares Manufacturers Association, 1973.

Leuchtenburg, William E. *The Perils of Prosperity, 1914–1932.* Chicago: University of Chicago Press, 1958.

Magic Chef, Inc. Board Minutes, 1961–1985.

McElvaine, Robert S. *The Great Depression: America, 1929–1941.* New York: Times Books, 1984.

Proctor, William. *The Templeton Touch.* New York: Doubleday & Company, 1983.

Rybcznski, Witold. *Home: A Short History of an Idea.* New York: Viking, 1986.

Rymer, S. B., Jr. "The Magic Chef Story." Address to the Newcomen Society, Cleveland, 1979.

Sanders, Clyde A. and Dudley C. Gould. *History Cast in Metals.* Des Plaines, Illinois: American Foundrymen's Society, 1976.

Simpson, Bruce. *History of the Metalcasting Industry.* Des Plaines, Illinois: American Foundrymen's Society, 1948.

Schonberger, Richard J. *World Class Manufacturing: The Lessons of Simplicity Applied.* New York: The Free Press, 1986.

Stevenson, Jordan & Harrison, Inc. "General Summary Dixie Dealer Division Sales Problems and Procedures." 1952.

Snell, William R. *Cleveland the Beautiful: A History of Cleveland, Tennessee, 1842–1931.* np, 1986.

Strasser, Susan. *Never Done: A History of American Housework.* New York: Pantheon, 1982.

Index